The Authorities

Powerful Wisdom from Leaders in the Field

SARAH Y GOFF

Award Winning Author

Publisher
Authorities Press
Markham, ON
Canada

Printed in the United States, Canada, and the United Kingdom.

FOREWORD

Experts are to be admired for their knowledge, but they often remain unrecognized by the general public because they save their information and insights for paying customers and clients. There are many experts in a given field, but their impact is limited to the handful of people with whom they work.

Unlike experts, authorities share their knowledge and expertise far more broadly, so they make a big impact on the world. Authorities become known and admired as leading experts and, as such, typically do very well economically and professionally. Most authorities are also mature enough to know that part of the joy of monetary success is the accompanying moral and spiritual obligation to give back.

Many people want to learn and work with well-respected and generous authorities, but don't always know where to find them. They may be known to their peers, or within a specific community, but have not had the opportunity to reach a wider audience. At one time, they might have submitted a proposal to the *For Dummies* or *Chicken Soup for the Soul series* of books, but it's now almost impossible to get accepted as a new author in such a branded book series.

It is more than fitting that Raymond Aaron, an internationally known and respected authority in his own right, would be the one to recognize the need for a new venue in which authorities could share their considerable knowledge with readers everywhere. As the only author ever to be included in both of the book series mentioned above, Raymond has had the opportunity to give back and he understands how crucial it is for authorities to have a platform from which to share their expertise.

I

I have known and worked with Raymond for a number of years and consider him a valued friend and talented coach. He knows how to spot talented and knowledgeable people and he desires to see them prosper. Over the years, success coaching and speaking engagements around the world have made it possible for Raymond to meet many of these talented authorities. He recognizes and relates to their passion and enthusiasm for what they do, as well as their desire to share what they know. He tells me that's why he has created this new nonfiction branded book series, *The Authorities*.

Dr. Nido Qubein
President, High Point University

TABLE OF CONTENTS

IV

INTRODUCTION

Welcome to *The Authorities*. This is an anthology of stories and ideas from individuals who have distinguished themselves in life and in business. They are people who leave big footprints on the world, and as leaders in their particular fields they also understand the importance and obligation of giving something back.

Authorities are not just experts. They are individuals who are also known to be outstanding in their fields and in their communities. Because they are esteemed and distinguished in both realms, Authorities are able to significantly impact humanity through their chosen work, their life of service, and their contributions toward creating lasting change.

The featured author is Sarah Y Goff and her unique gift to the business world, an algorithm for launching your digital business or for taking your existing business into the heady virtual marketplace. Sarah's *Entrepreneur's Quick Start Guide to Building a Digital Sales Machine* is chock full of information that has proven to be useful in building her own multi-million-dollar Digital Sales Machine (DSM) and you can benefit from her meteoric ascension in this unlikeliest of arenas.

From assembling the elements crucial to your success as a digital entrepreneur to the actual conversion of leads into customers, Sarah walks you through each important step in the creation of your DSM. Developing the right mindset, automating and delegating, advertising in the correct way—these are just some of the topics you must consider when building a DSM, and they're part of Sarah's effort to include you in a movement toward a better way of doing business, a better way of being a citizen of the world.

Consider her mission to share the pieces of the puzzle to representing a successful digital business and the basic advice she offers to everyone involved in the digital marketplace. "Think big (and beyond your means) to provide value to others," she says. "This will, in turn, bring great rewards."

Stated clearly, Sarah's vision is to deliver value to the masses and bring together like-minded entrepreneurs and businesspeople, creating a movement that elevates creators of breakthrough ideas, tips and strategies who are willing to share for the benefit of society.

Sarah's mother came from Trinidad and her father from Malaysia in the late sixties—both parents were seeking bigger opportunities. Her parents started their nursing training with the NHS and settled in the UK to start a family, with Sarah and her two brothers. They literally came with a suitcase and some money in their back pocket. Educating yourself was of huge importance in Sarah's life. She was told to learn a skill; no one can take that away from you.

Born in the United Kingdom with two siblings, Sarah Y Goff lived in Surrey in a family of five. She followed the traditional educational path—school, college, university and post-graduate diploma, then continued to gain further professional qualifications in marketing.

Sarah spent 20 years in a corporate 9-5 job in marketing in financial services. Various marketing-related roles and responsibilities included corporate event planning and retail design. In December 2016 she was made redundant and became a Digital Entrepreneur. Since then, she has built a successful, multi-million-dollar, working side-by-side with her husband and business partner to build an online business from scratch.

When questioned about becoming an entrepreneur, Sarah says that during the first two years she feels like she has educated herself, cramming in ten years worth of learning in a short space of time. In her early twenties, Sarah studied marketing as a profession. She did a few courses as part of her corporate job, but nothing more than that for nearly ten years in her thirties, as she fell in love, got married and had two kids. Instead of academic learning, she was learning life lessons being a wife and then a mother. Now in her forties and at the beginning of her entrepreneurial journey, her digital business is an exciting venture that has already begun to present major opportunities for growth and overall success.

Sarah is on a mission to discover and share the pieces to the puzzle that make for a successful digital business. We're each on our own journey to succeed— our own mission to share a message, and deliver and serve the masses while also looking to make the world a better place. Thinking big and beyond one's means to offer value to others first will, in turn, bring great rewards.

Sarah's vision is to deliver value to the masses and bring together like-minded entrepreneurs and those who want to be their own boss, to create a movement where elevating creators of breakthrough ideas, tips and strategies is shared in communities for all humanity to benefit.

Sarah enjoys spending time with her children and being able to watch them grow up and is grateful every day that she is living a freer life. A proud mother to Henry and Jasmine, she is married to her business partner, Chris. They split their time between their London home and their home in Florida.

Read each chapter in this anthology carefully to learn and to see the business possibilities that may exist between yourself and any of The Authorities. You could become their client or, perhaps, do business with them in other ways.

These are *The Authorities*. Learn from them. Connect with them. Let them uplift you. Learning from them and working with them is the secret ingredient for success which may well allow you to rise to the level of Authority soon.

To be considered for inclusion in a subsequent edition of *The Authorities*, register to attend an event at www.aaron.com/events where you will be interviewed and considered.

An Entrepreneur's Quick Start Guide to Building a Digital Sales Machine

SARAH Y GOFF

WHAT IS A DIGITAL SALES MACHINE (DSM)?

A DSM can be likened to a recipe, where each ingredient is carefully measured out and then added together in a specific order and particular method, to create a wonderful food experience. Some would also refer to it as an algorithm—a series of repeatable steps that lead to a consistent result.

You can't rush when following this recipe. Do so, and your dough may not rise. Knead too much, and it will become hard and unusable. Set the temperature too low, and you could be left with a sodden lump of partially cooked dough instead of a golden loaf of bread. Miss an ingredient or step, fail to measure accurately or forget to stir, and you'll end up with something inedible. It's true, if you proceed with care, due diligence and love when creating something in the kitchen, it will show in the end result. Similarly, failure to execute your DSM will lead to inconsistent results that might foreshadow the failure of the company. So, it's not always about what you do, it's the way you do it!

DSM EXAMPLE

An example of an ultimate sales machine is McDonald's, the world largest hamburger chain, serving 58 million customers daily. It controls the supplier chain—from growing ingredients, to processing them, to transporting them to the distribution centre and then finally into the designated restaurant. McDonald's has a proven system that they offer franchisees. Basically, it's a blueprint they can use to set up the local restaurant for the owner.

The company has also systematised their menu options into various steps that lead to an ordered process of events designed to achieve the chosen outcome. The system is highly automated, so employees literally press buttons to produce a standardized hamburger you can depend on, no matter where you are in the world. It's the recipe for success we were just talking about.

DSM ELEMENTS

When building a DSM, using the example of an ecommerce business, you need to consider different elements of what's required to make the business operate, and then attract customers to come and buy from you again and again. In this chapter, we'll explore those elements and how they come together to bring in people who repeatedly buy what you have to offer.

Legal and Compliance: This is a first and crucial step. Just to stick with the recipe concept for a little longer, it's like laying out all the quality ingredients you need to for your recipe as well as making sure you have the correct baking implements, and that your stove is preheated.

You'll begin by choosing and registering your company name, deciding if it will be a limited company, partnership or sole proprietorship, finding a location, building your website and understanding what content is needed to make you compliant to operate—such as privacy notice, terms of service, etc.

Payment Processes and Procedures: Extrapolating further from our recipe concept, this is akin to choosing the presentation plate(s), china and silverware. And it's about placement, deciding whether you'll allow guests to browse the baking selection or just serve them at the table. You'll also need to determine how you'll integrate this with the rest of the meal or event.

In other words: How will your customers purchase from you? How will you capture the payments? Will you offer your customers multiple payment options, and what will they be? How will they all integrate with your store set up?

Marketing: This is where you'll define for yourself the person who's going to be consuming what you bake. You'll need to ask questions about demographics, their likes and dislikes and even whether or not they're allergic to the ingredients you've selected. What can you do to make sure the product appeals to your guests? How will the offering appear on the menu? You'll even have to consider the invitation or advertisement of your event. And here's an interesting question—do the guests know you, your cooking and your reputation?

Let's put this in actual business terms. How will you promote the products you develop? Who are you selling to? Who is your customer avatar (a representation of your ideal customer)? Do you understand your customer avatar's pain points, desires and needs? How will you communicate the reasons why you should be their solution? And probably most important, how is it that your customer avatar knows, likes and trusts you before buying (this links into your brand).

Sourcing Products: As you can see our idea of a recipe has morphed completely into the idea of an actual business product. Where will you source your components or products? Remember to complete due diligence for counterfeit items that could be detrimental to your brand. How do you know what to sell? Are you going to offer evergreen or seasonal products or both? What prices are you going to set?

Personnel and Virtual Assistants: As an entrepreneur, you need to wear all hats when you start off, and it can be overwhelming. You should be prepared to outsource and delegate as you may not have the skills or time to carry out tasks like bookkeeping and accounting. Who will deal with the touch points affecting your customer as they journey through your DSM?

Technology: What technical platforms will you choose for your store? Which apps will you select to help you operate your ecommerce business? Are there outside platforms you'll need to integrate with your ecommerce solution? Make sure all programs are compatible and talking to each other correctly.

Suppliers and Vendors: Find good reliable suppliers or vendors you can trust. Building good relationships is crucial to your success. Identify what steps you'll need to take to build customer relationships to the point where they not only know you but also like and trust you. Recognize that this will take time, commitment and effort on your part.

Brand: You'll need to have a brand name, logo, fonts and colours, and develop unique positioning and a personality that stands out from the crowd, otherwise you'll fail to attract customers. It's important to understand that branding is linked to marketing (some consider it a subset) and should not be confused with sales. The term sales references all activities that lead to the selling of goods and services, while marketing is the process of getting people interested in the goods and services being sold. Another way of putting this is that marketing is about laying the groundwork for sales.

My business partner (and husband) Chris Goff has developed a metaphor for branding known as The Coffee Cup Analogy. It says that brand is a cup of coffee. Why coffee? When I referred to branding as a cup of coffee, a picture should have formed in your mind of a steaming mug of fresh ground, percolated Arabica or perhaps Sumatra. Maybe it was a latte or an expresso, or a picture of what you drink instead of coffee. The point is that everyone has a different mental picture of what coffee means to them, based on their life experience. That's brand.

Brand relates to your business in that you're trying to elicit a common response across a wide variety of people—your customer base. Companies like Apple and people like Sir Richard Branson have done this impeccably. You would do well to study examples of your favourite businesses, products and people to see just what they've done and how.

Social Media Platforms - Communication Channels: Which social media platform will you focus on and master first? We're talking about places like Facebook, Twitter, Instagram, Pinterest and YouTube. Are you going to approach this with the idea of becoming an influencer or is it just a means to an end? Remember that when you start off things may appear to be a disaster before you become a master. That's why it's important to choose one skill to master before learning another. An important business concept to learn is the habit of focusing on one thing at a time, according to priority (look up the Ivy Lee Method).

Advertising: On which social platform(s) will you choose to advertise? How will you identify and target these platforms? Repeated testing, and trial and error are important parts of making your DSM work. It's always a good idea to run two ads at a time, one that's proven and one that you're trying out. Discover and feed the machine with the right information and it will produce the desired results.

Investment: It will cost you time and money at the outset to make the DSM work. You'll also have to demonstrate commitment and consistency over the long-term to succeed. Building a DSM is not an overnight task, it will take about 18 months to two years to launch it, which you can maintain and improve on. More on this later.

MAKING THE DIGITAL LEAP

Why are all the DSM elements important? They'll help you form that recipe, the algorithm or set of steps you can take, to increase your chances of creating a successful digital business. You'll be building a 'process' that creates effective output of the desired results. What might those results be, in terms of profit or Return on Investment (ROI)? Typically, a DSM should return $2 for every $1 invested.

What will happen if you don't create the perfect recipe? Business failure statistics reveal that brick and mortar stores face incredible odds. It's worse for those that attempt to make the switch to digital operations.

Currently, The U.S. Bureau of Labour Statistics (BLS) indicates that 20% of new businesses fail during the first two years of being open, 45% during the first five years and 65% during the first 10 years. Only 25% of new businesses make it to 15 years or more.

Consider that a massive 73 percent of enterprises failed to provide any business value whatsoever from their digital transformation efforts, according to a 2018 study by the Everest Group. And 78 percent failed to meet their business objectives. Scary. Especially when well-known companies like GE, Lego, Nike, Procter & Gamble, Burberry and Ford have experienced embarrassing reversals when attempting to cross the digital gulf.

So, if the odds aren't in your favour, why do you need a DSM in your life right now? It's kind of a Catch 22 situation: those who fail to actuate a DSM for their business will have perpetual time, financial and location limitations. But by far the strongest reason for creating a DSM is the fact that once it's up and running, you'll have an automated system for making money. That's right, you'll have the ability to make money while you sleep! It ties into the ideas presented by Robert Kiyosaki in his Cashflow Quadrant...

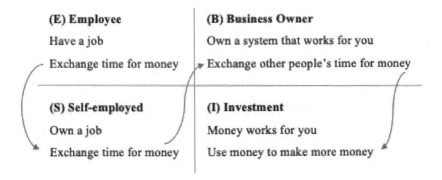

(E) Employee	(B) Business Owner
Have a job	Own a system that works for you
Exchange time for money	Exchange other people's time for money
(S) Self-employed	(I) Investment
Own a job	Money works for you
Exchange time for money	Use money to make more money

Quadrant One (E): You're an Employee programmed to go to grade school, college or university and get a job. You have a job where you trade time for money.

Quadrant Two (S): You're Self-employed. You own a job, but you still trade time for money.

Quadrant Three (B): You're a Business Owner. You own a system or process, and people work for you to create money. You still invest some time, but you can make money while you sleep. Note: successful business owners strive to find ways to buy more time, whilst there is an abundance of people willing to sell their time for money. Sad truth.

Quadrant Four (I): You're an Investor. You own investments that work for you, even while you sleep.

To build wealth, you ideally want to work from quadrant one through to quadrant four. Why you need to be on the right side of the box? Taking the risk gives you time, financial freedom and location freedom. 90% of people fall into the left-side quadrants and have 10% of the wealth. 10% of the people fall into the right-side quadrants and have 90% of the wealth.

Stop Renting Your Life and Own Your Life!

Being a digital entrepreneur and a mom of two young children, freeing up time to be present in their lives as they grow up is extremely important to me. Because of this I chose to live my life by taking the risk to move from the left-hand side quadrants to the right-hand side quadrants, creating the potential to earn income to live a life I could never reach being stuck in the employee quadrant. Before becoming a digital entrepreneur, I never even knew about the quadrants.

I don't want to be the too-tired parent unable to be involved with my whole heart and soul in whatever exciting news my son or daughter must tell me right there and then. Or worse, staying late at the office and then commuting the long journey back home—only to find my children already in bed asleep.

I see so many of my colleagues experience this, and they are so grateful for school holidays so they can spend a fixed amount of time with their kids.

What parent doesn't want to spend quality time with their family and close ones? I spent 20 years of my life programmed to be an employee as the path to success. It was a case of you don't know what you don't know. Now I know ... and now I'm thinking big.

We all comment how time flies by too quickly. Well, as a mother of two young kids the days are long, but the years are short. If you aren't living in the present, this will happen time and time again. So, to enjoy your days and years, you may want to stop renting your life and start living the time you have on this planet before it's too late.

When is it Too Late?

It's too late when you had the chance to do it and didn't. It's also too late when you have the chance to do it and can't.

HOW TO BUILD A DSM

You need to have a blueprint for your DSM, which will enable you to design with the big picture in mind. It's a planning tool outlining a framework of key components necessary to build consistency and reach and complete each stage of the process.

Traffic: You need traffic to fuel your DSM. This is where you promote and attract quality leads for your funnel. One of the social media giants of our generation is the Facebook communication channel, with the ability to create laser-targeted advertising campaigns using the wealth of data Facebook has on its users. It's an advertiser's dream come true, if used correctly to leverage its sheer power of finding the right audience to place in front of the right product at the right time.

Facebook offers support to help advertisers use their platform. They do so because they want you to succeed so you continue to spend with them. It's a WIN-WIN situation.

Funnel: It's crucial to optimize your funnel so that your conversion rate is as close to 100 as possible. Every increase in your conversion rate means more sales for you. Find who's doing this well in your industry and model from it. There's no need to reinvent the wheel when you've got a fast-track hack right there for you. I would go so far as purchasing their product or service, studying it and then modelling what you learn.

Front End: Create an irresistible offer your customers can't ignore. Attract your target audience through their desires or pain points, make your promotional copy 'speak to them,' have emotive triggers to entice your target audience into taking action and give them your best email to bridge ongoing communications as they subscribe into your brand. The bottom line is they must perceive there's something of value to them or they won't act.

Split Test: Building a DSM requires constant fine tuning as you improve and widen your horizon of target audiences and understand their other desires and pain points. Think big. If your target audience has opted to purchase a kitchen gadget because they're struggling to open a ring-pulled can, what else could they be struggling with in life? What value can you offer that they'll respond too? For example, you can cross over to other industries with useful products. People with arthritis will appreciate useful beauty products, certain bedroom and bathroom items and even garden tools, designed with them in mind. Create a template that works for this type of target audience, build up a customer avatar and identify all their desires and pain points. Try different angles for the same offer—alternate variations of the same advertisement—to your target audience. Test, test, test to discover the honey holes of untapped gaps in the market.

Back End Communication: Once you've engaged with your customers, don't stop. You need to think long-term with acquisition of customers who seek value from their initial investment and keep attracting them to your various offers and consciously build brand loyalty. It's all about retention and open communication channels. One traditional, and still effective, key communication method is email marketing; it's how you can literally turn on the tap and squeeze value from the prospects and clients you've already warmed up, by continuing to serve them with beneficial offerings that are relevant to them.

HOW TO GLUE THE PARTS OF YOUR DSM TOGETHER

Everything is mindset when running a business. Yes, you need to invest, build skills, develop know how and put the right components into place, but regardless of where your starting point is, your risk perspective is going to have to be rewired. Being a corporate employee for 20 years kept me safe and secure in the predictable receipt of a monthly pay cheque. I say this because not being exposed to risk has a conditioning effect, in that fear will tend to keep you from doing anything outside of your normal environment. So, transforming from employee to entrepreneur is a leap of faith; you're jumping into the unknown without a safety net and hoping you land on your feet. Also consider that as an employee, your actions don't usually have a direct impact on the bottom line, but that as an entrepreneur, everything you do and don't do directly impacts the bottom line—the buck stops with you. Mindset makes the difference! As Henry Ford said, "Whether you can or you can't you are right."

The pressure on an entrepreneur is immense, especially when you're first starting out, yet the excitement and the potential to earn big drives you forward. However, what can happen when you've been an entrepreneur for a period of time and haven't achieved what you intended, is that you start to feel frustrated … like a failure … embarrassed to have a business that's going nowhere fast … stuck. This is where the right mindset can help push you on through to preserve your business goals. It can help you to develop a solid reason as to WHY you need to take action. It not only assures you'll benefit but that the people closest to you will benefit as well.

Sometimes the thought of quitting isn't an option, so you carry on. You do this because you never know if the next best idea is just around the corner, or if your new business strategy is going to be the one that gives you the breakthrough you needed.

Winners never quit, quitters never win. – Vince Lombardi

And sometimes, when you don't have anything else left to grasp, you just have to believe and have faith that you'll make things work in your business.

It always seems impossible until it's done. – Nelson Mandela

Other traits can come into play as you reach low points in your business and are facing challenge after challenge. These motivators allow you to rise up each time to overcome—to survive. For example, a mentor will offer guidance and help you to develop a sense of not being alone in business. And even if you're the only person in your business, there are forums where you can talk with others like you. This is why it's important to join groups in your niche. You'll be surprised how easy it is to find a close network you can tap into, where ideas and tips can be shared with one another. There are so many communities you can join where you can share thoughts and benefit from the personal experiences of others who are like you. I also believe that when someone has been where you are now, and they offer to help, the entrepreneurial world becomes a better place.

DIGITAL TOOLS

Automate and Delegate: When you build the system and it works, it's time to automate and delegate. It's important to recognize and reach this stage so you can stop working in your business and start working on your business—to grow and scale it.

Benefits of Automation:

- Invest time now to automate processes so that you'll save time later

- Set it up once and let it run itself

- Passively earn income

- Fine tune to maximize output

How to Automate:

- Identify activities that are repetitive and systematize them

- Identify activities that follow a pattern flow and create an algorithm

- Identify activities that can form a predictable sequence and develop procedures to make them autonomous

Why Should You Automate:

- Saves you time in the future

- Allows you to focus on growing your business

- More efficient and consistent output

Examples of What to Automate:

- Customer Service replies (broken, never received, etc.)

- Product-specific questions (size, colour variations, etc.)

- Discount replies (fence sitters to convert)

- Email Building List replies (build your list)

- Fan Page replies (grab a fan)

What Happens if You Can't Automate:

- You need to delegate the task to a Virtual Assistant

- Have your tasks and processes clearly documented

- Go to the recruitment marketplace to search for suitable candidates

- Interview candidates

- Select the candidate that matches your business needs

- Nurture this resource and build a relationship with them, and they'll reward you with loyalty and willingness to do their best

- Everyone is a winner

HOW TO OPERATE YOUR DSM

Set the Objectives: What do you want to achieve? Generate awareness (build your brand and generate leads) and explain each objective.

Test, Test, Test: Check each component of your machine against real world conditions.

HOW DO YOU MAKE CONVERSIONS HAPPEN?

Scarcity: When you add scarcity to your business offer, it taps into the Fear of Missing Out (FOMO)—a feeling of if I don't take this offer now, I may not get a chance later and someone else will take my place. Most people have a mindset of scarcity rather than a mindset of abundance. Lead to engage in the here and now, before it's gone. This sense of scarcity can be achieved by showing the difference between XX quantity bought and XX quantity left. Also look for advertising copy like "Limited spaces left!" or "Act now to avoid disappointment."

Urgency: When you add urgency to your business offer, this taps into the fear of missing out FOMO again, and it encourages your customer to act now and not to leave it to do later, which generally does not happen because life gets in the way. Once you've engaged a lead to your business offer, you must aim to get them to act now and quickly. Letting it wait until later results in a warmed-up lead going cold. You want every investment made to acquire a lead to your business offer matter and to convert to the action you intended. That is, to engage with your business offer.

Value: When what you're offering gives perceived value to your target audience, that offer becomes attractive to the right leads, who are likely to convert into buyers. When your content isn't appealing to your target audience or you find your leads don't move further into your sales funnel, this usually means the value of your content is no longer resonating with your target audience. Producing above and beyond valuable content on a consistent basis will retain a steady flow of fresh new and existing leads warmed for when you want to put a new business offer in front of them. For example, providing direct contact with your audience, live or pre-recorded, keeps your personal or business brand front of mind. Offering value on a regular basis trains your target audience to 'tune in' to what you have to say, which is a good way to position yourself or your business offer.

Free Content: Offering free content is a popular way to attract initial interest to your business offer. This works well when you follow up on the free content using an email auto responder, which is essentially a sequence for keeping initial leads warmed up and ready to view your core business offering. In a sales funnel, the free content is usually in exchange for an email address, which gives you implicit permission to write to the person regarding future business offers. Building an email list is an essential function of a DSM as it is one of your key business assets.

Budget: When you have a DSM that's generating revenue, there's no budget; you just feed it what it needs, whilst making your fine-tuning adjustments to see what works and what doesn't. Sooner or later, you'll make an adjustment to the DSM that will send your revenue through the roof. Until then, revert to the original state and keep testing!

MAINTENANCE: HOW TO KEEP YOUR DSM FINE-TUNED

Keeping Up to Date with Industry Knowledge: Even though you may have automated your business and delegated daily tasks, and you're earning passive income from it, this doesn't mean you forget about it completely. You always need to fine tune it as market and customer needs change. If you become complacent with your business, you're neglecting the inevitable event of change. Even the biggest brands dominating their industry get caught out and lose market share. An example here is Apple, they have a loyal following but have become complacent about listening to their customers' needs. The basic functions of the iPhone are being affected by overall low battery life, despite daily charging. A basic and minimum expectation is to have a workable battery for operating your smart phone. Now customers are seeking other brands that will offer them what they need.

Reinvest into the DSM: When you first start to see profit generated from your DSM, you need to reinvest and keep on feeding it. Keep the momentum going, since once it starts you can't suddenly put the emergency handbrake on. You must keep the engine running and see where it takes you, working on the motor until it becomes fine-tuned to the point where the more fuel you put into it the more it will produce for you. The feeling you'll get when you have a well fine-tuned DSM is the natural high of being an entrepreneur running a business that can't be stopped.

Optimize All Aspects of the DSM and Check for Leakages: Turn up the volume, scale your DSM and make more money. Get more affiliates and influencers to see your digital assets via bloggers, email lists, YouTube, Facebook, LinkedIn, WhatsApp, Snapchat, etc. Seek them out to promote your digital presence. Fill your pipeline every day with two to three influencers of 20 to 30 people. Convince people to say "Yes." You should be looking for a conversion rate of at least 10%. Repeat this process over and over again.

Domino Effect: Ask affiliates to do a testimonial video. That way customers don't just hear it from you, they hear from someone else who has had success. Leverage these testimonials.

Troubleshooting: Being an entrepreneur can be a lonely place, but I assure you there are others just like you who have a passion and the drive to succeed. These are people with whom you can share tips, hacks and ideas that may help your business and vice versa. They can be found online and off, on social platforms and in your local chamber of commerce, so keep your eyes and ears open and prevail.

And now, here we are at the end of our time together. We've discussed a great deal in just a few pages. What follows is a short summary of our discussions and a link to further information...

SUMMARY: HOW TO BUILD A DSM

1. Study successful DSMs

2. Assemble the necessary elements

3. Make the digital leap

4. Follow your blueprint

5. Develop the right mindset

6. Automate and delegate

7. Start operations

8. Begin converting leads into customers

9. Maintain and fine-tune your DSM

To discover more about how Sarah Y Goff has succeeded in the digital world please connect with her at: https://www.facebook.com/iamsarahygoff

Step Into Greatness

LES BROWN

You have greatness within you. You can do more than you could ever imagine. The problem most people have is that they set a goal and then ask, "how can I do it? I don't have the necessary skills or education or experience."

I know what that's like. I wasted 14 years on asking myself how I could be a motivational speaker. My mind focused on the negative—on the things that were in my way, rather than on the things that were not.

It's not what you don't have but what you think you need that keeps you from getting what you want from life. But, when the dream is big enough, the obstacles don't matter. You'll get there if you stay the course. Nothing can stop you but death itself.

Think about that last statement for a minute. There's nothing on this earth that can stop you from achieving what it is that you want. So, get out of your way, and quit sabotaging your dreams. Do everything in your power to make them happen—because you cannot fail!

They say the best way to die is with your loved ones gathered around your bed. But what if you were dying and it was the ideas you never acted upon, the gifts you never used and the dreams you never pursued, that were circled around your bed? Answer that question right now. Write down your answers. If you die this very moment, what ideas, what gifts, what dreams will die with you?

Then say: I refuse to die an unlived life! You beat out 40 million sperm to get here, and you'll never have to face such odds again. Walk through the field of life and leave a trail behind.

One day, one of my rich friends brought my mother a new pair of shoes for me. Now, even though we weren't well off, I didn't want them; they were a size nine and I was a size nine and a half. My mother didn't listen and told my sister to go get some Vaseline, which she rubbed all over my feet. Then my mother had me put those shoes on, minding that I didn't scrunch down the heel. She had my sister run some water in the bathtub, and I was told to get in and walk around in the water. I said that my feet hurt. She just ignored me and asked about my day at school, how everything went and did I get into any fights? I knew what she was up to, that she was trying to distract me, so I said I had only gotten into three fights. After a while mother asked me if my feet still hurt. I admitted that the pain had indeed lessened. She kept me walking in that tub until I had a brand new pair of comfortable, size nine and a half shoes.

You see, once the leather in the shoes got wet, they stretched! And what you need to do is stretch a little. I believe that most people don't set high goals and miss them, but rather, they set lower goals and hit them and then they stay there, stuck on the side of the highway of life. When you're pursuing your greatness, you don't know what your limitations are, and you need to act like you don't have any. If you shoot for the moon and miss, you'll still be in the stars.

You also need coaching (a mentor). Why? There are times you, too, will find yourself parked on the side of the highway of life with no gas in the vehicle. What you need then is someone to stop and offer to pick up some gas down the road a ways and bring it back to you. That person is your coach. Yes, they are there for advice, but their main job is to help you through the difficulties that life throws at all of us.

Another reason for having a coach is that you can't see the picture when you're in the frame. In other words, he or she can often see where you are with a clarity and focus that's unavailable to you. They're not going to leave you parked along the road of life, nor are they going to allow you to be stuck in the moment like a photo in a frame.

And let's say you just can't see your way forward. You don't believe it's possible. Sometimes you just have to believe in someone's belief in you. This could be your coach, a loved one, or even a staunch friend. You need to hear them say you can do it, time and again. Because, after all, faith comes from hearing and hearing and hearing.

Look at it this way. Most people fail because of possibility blindness. They can't see what lies before them. There are always possibilities. Because of this, your dream is possible. You may fail often. In fact, I want you to say this: I will fail my way to success. Here is why.

I had a TV show that failed. I felt I had to go back to public speaking. I had failed, so I parked my car for 10 years. Then I saw Dr. Wayne Dyer was still on PBS and I decided to call them. They said they would love to work with me and asked where I had been. I wasn't as good as I had been 10 years before, as I was out of practice, but I still had to get back in the game. I was determined to drive on empty.

Listen to recordings, go to seminars, challenge yourself, and you'll begin to step into your greatness; you'll begin to fill yourself with the energy you need to climb to greater heights. Most people never attend a seminar. They won't invest money in books or audio programs. You put yourself in the top five percent just by making a different choice than the average person. This is called contrary thinking. It's a concept taken from the financial industry. One considers choosing the exact opposite behaviour of the average person as a way to get better than average results. You don't have to make the contrarian choice, but if you don't have anything to lose by going that road, why not consider the option?

Make your move before you're ready. Walk by faith, not by sight, and make sure you're happy doing it. If you can't be happy, what else is there? Helen Keller said, "Life is short, eat the dessert first."

What is faith? Many of us think of God when we think of faith. A different viewpoint claims that faith is a firm belief in something for which there is no proof. I would rather think of faith as something that is believed especially with strong conviction. It is this last definition I am referring to when I say walk by faith, not by sight. Be happy and go forth with strong conviction that you are destined for greatness.

An important step on your way to greatness is to take the time to detoxify. You've got to look at the people in your life. What are they doing for you? Are they setting a pace that you can follow? If not, whose pace have you adjusted to? If you're the smartest in your group, find a new group.

Are the people in your life pulling you down or lifting you up? You know what to do, right? Banish the negative and stay with the positive; it's that simple. Dr. Norman Vincent Peale once said (when I was in the audience), "You are special. You have greatness within you, and you can do more than you could ever possibly imagine."

He overrode the inner conversations in my mind and reached the heart of me. He set me on fire. This is yet another reason for seeking out the help of a coach or mentor, or other new people in your life. They can do what Dr. Peale did for me. They can set your passion free.

How important is it to have the right kind of person/people on your side? There was a study done that determined it takes 16 people saying you can do something to overcome one person who says you can't do something. That's right, one negative, unsupportive person can wipe out the work of 16 other supportive people. The message can't be any clearer than that.

Let's face the cold, hard truth: most people stay in park along the highway of life. They never feel the passion, the love for their fellow man, or for the work they do. They are stuck in the proverbial rut. What's the reason? There are many reasons, but only one common factor: fear—fear of change, fear of failure, fear of success, fear they may not be good enough, fear of competition, even fear of rejection.

"Rejection is a myth," says Jack Canfield, co-author of The Chicken Soup for the Soul series. "It's not like you get a slap in the face each time you are rejected." Why not take every "no" you receive as a vitamin, and every time you take one, know you are another step closer to success.

You will win if you don't quit. Even a broken clock is right twice a day.

Professional baseball players, on average, get on base just three times out of every 10 times they face the opposing pitcher. Even superstars fail half of the time they appear at the plate.

Top commissioned salespeople face similar odds. They may make one sale from every three people they see, but it will have taken them between 75 and 100 telephone calls to make the 15 appointments they need to close their five sales for the week. And these are statistics for the elite. Most salespeople never reach these kinds of numbers.

People don't spend their lives working for just one company anymore. This means you must build up a set of skills and experiences that are portable. This can be done a number of ways, but my favorite approaches follow.

You must be willing to do the things others won't do, in order to have tomorrow the things that others don't have. Provide more service than you get paid for. Set some high standards for yourself.

Begin each day with your most difficult task. The rest of the day will seem more enjoyable and a whole lot easier.

Someone needs help with a problem? Be the solution to that problem.

Also, find those tasks that are being consistently ignored and do them. You'll be surprised by the results. An acquaintance of mine used this approach at a number of entry-level positions and each time he quickly ended up being offered a position in management.

You must increase your energy. Kick it up a notch. We are spirits having a physical existence; let your spirit shine. Quit frittering away your energy. Use it to move you closer to the achievement of your dreams. Refuse to spend it on non-productive activities.

What do people say about you when you leave a room? Are you willing to take responsibility—to walk your talk. There is a terrible epidemic sweeping our nation, and it is the refusal to take responsibility for one's actions. Consider that at some point in any situation there will have been a moment where you could have done something to change the outcome. To that end, you are responsible for what happened. It's a hard thing to accept, but it's true.

Life's hard. It was hard when I was told I had cancer. I had sunken into despair, and was hiding away in my study when my son came in. My son asked me if I was going to die. What could I do? I told him I was going to fight, even though I was scared. I also told him that I needed some help. Not because I was weak, but because I wanted to stay strong. Keep asking until you get help. Don't stop until you get it.

A setback is the setup for a comeback. A setback is simply a misstep on the long road of success. It means nothing in the larger scheme of things. And, surprisingly, it sets you up for your next win. It tends to focus you and your energy on your immediate goals, paving the way for your next sprint, for your comeback.

It's worth it. Your dreams are worth the sacrifices you'll have to make to achieve them. Find five reasons that will make your dreams worth it for you. Say to yourself, I refuse to live an unlived life.

If you are casual about your dreams, you'll end up a casualty. You must be passionate about your dreams, living and breathing them throughout your days. You've got to be hungry! People who are hungry refuse to take no for an answer. Make NO your vitamin. Be unstoppable. Be hungry.

Let me give you an example of what I mean by hungry …

I decided I wanted to become a disc jockey, so I went down to the local radio station and asked the manager, Mr. Milton "Butterball" Smith, if he had a job available for a disc jockey. He said he did not. The next day I went back, and Mr. Smith asked, "Weren't you here yesterday?" I explained that I was just checking to see if anyone was sick or had died. He responded by telling me not to come back again. Day three, I went back again—with the same story. Mr. Smith told me to get out of there. I came back the fourth day and gave Mr. Smith my story one more time. He was so beside himself that he told me to get him a cup of coffee. I said, "Yes, sir!" That's how I became the errand boy.

While working as an errand boy at the station, I took every opportunity to hang out with the disc jockeys and to observe them working. After I had taught myself how to run the control room, it was just a matter of biding my time.

Then one day an opportunity presented itself. One of the disc jockeys by the name of Rockin' Roger was drinking heavily while he was on the air. It was a Saturday afternoon. And there I was, the only one there.

I watched him through the control-room window. I walked back and forth in front of that window like a cat watching a mouse, saying "Drink, Rock, Drink!" I was young. I was ready. And I was hungry.

Pretty soon, the phone rang. It was the station manager. He said, "Les, this is Mr. Klein."

I said, "Yes, I know."

He said, "Rock can't finish his program."

I said, "Yes sir, I know."

He said, "Would you call one of the other disc jockeys to fill in?"

I said, "Yes sir, I sure will, sir."

And when he hung up, I said, "Now he must think I'm crazy." I called up my mama and my girlfriend, Cassandra, and I told them, "Ya'll go out on the front porch and turn up the radio, I'M ABOUT TO COME ON THE AIR!"

I waited 15 or 20 minutes and called the station manager back. I said, "Mr. Klein, I can't find NOBODY!"

He said, "Young boy, do you know how to work the controls?"

I said, "Yes, sir."

He said, "Go in there, but don't say anything. Hear me?"

I said, "Yes, sir."

I couldn't wait to get old Rock out of the way. I went in there, took my seat behind that turntable, flipped on the microphone, and let 'er rip.

"Look out, this is me, LB., triple P. Les Brown your platter-playin' papa. There were none before me and there will be none after me, therefore that makes me the one and only. Young and single and love to mingle, certified, bona fide, and indubitably qualified to bring you satisfaction and a whole lot of action. Look out baby, I'm your LOVE man."

I WAS HUNGRY!

During my adult life, I've been a disc jockey, a radio station manager, a Democrat in the Ohio Legislature, a minister, a TV personality, an author, and a public speaker, but I've always looked after what I valued most—my mother. What I want for her is one of my dreams, one of my goals.

My life has been a true testament to the power of positive thinking and the infinite human potential. I was born in an abandoned building on a floor in Liberty City, a low-income section of Miami, Florida, and adopted at six weeks of age by Mrs. Mamie Brown, a 38-year-old single woman, cafeteria cook, and domestic worker. She had very little education or financial means, but a very big heart and the desire to care for myself and my twin brother. I call myself Mrs. Mamie Brown's Baby Boy and I say that all that I am and all that I ever hoped to be, I owe to my mother.

My determination and persistence in searching for ways to help my mother overcome poverty, and developing my philosophy to do whatever it takes to achieve success, led me to become a distinguished authority on harnessing human potential and success. That philosophy is best expressed by the following …

> "If you want a thing bad enough to go out and fight for it,
> to work day and night for it,
> to give up your time, your peace, and your sleep for it…
> if all that you dream and scheme is about it,
> and life seems useless and worthless without it…
> if you gladly sweat for it and fret for it and plan for it
> and lose all your terror of the opposition for it…
> if you simply go after that thing you want
> with all of your capacity, strength, and sagacity,
> faith, hope and confidence and stern pertinacity…
> if neither cold, poverty, famine, nor gout,
> sickness nor pain, of body, and brain,
> can keep you away from the thing that you want…
> if dogged and grim you beseech and beset it,
> with the help of God, you will get it!"

Happiness: How to Experience the "Real Deals"

MARCI SHIMOFF

I was 41 years old, stretched out on a lounge chair by my pool and reflecting on my life. I had achieved all that I thought I needed to be happy.

You see, when I was a child, I thought there would be five main things that would ensure that I'd be happy: a successful career helping people, a loving husband, a comfortable home, a great body, and a wonderful circle of friends. After years of study, hard work, and a few "lucky breaks," I finally had them all. (Okay, so my body didn't quite look like Halle Berry's—but four out of five isn't bad!) You think I'd have been on the top of the world.

But surprisingly I wasn't. I felt an emptiness inside that the outer successes of life couldn't fill. I was also afraid that if I lost any of those things, I might be miserable. Sadly, I knew I wasn't alone in feeling this way.

While happiness is the one thing we all truly want, so few people really experience the deep and lasting fulfillment that fills our soul. Why aren't we finding it?

Because, in the words of the old country western song, we're looking for happiness in "all the wrong places."

Looking around, I saw that the happiest people I knew weren't the most successful and famous. Some were married, some were single. Some had lots of money, and some didn't have a dime. Some of them even had health challenges. From where I stood, there seemed to be no rhyme or reason to what made people happy. The obvious question became: *Could a person actually be happy for no reason?*

I had to find out.

So I threw myself into the study of happiness. I interviewed scores of scientists, as well as 100 unconditionally happy people. (I call them the Happy 100.) I delved into the research from the burgeoning field of positive psychology, the study of the positive traits that enable people to enjoy meaningful, fulfilling, and happy lives.

What I found changed my life. To share this knowledge with others, I wrote a book called *Happy for No Reason: 7 Steps to Being Happy from the Inside Out*.

One day, as I sat down to compile my findings, all the pieces of the puzzle fell into place. I had a simple, but profound "a-ha"—there's a continuum of happiness.

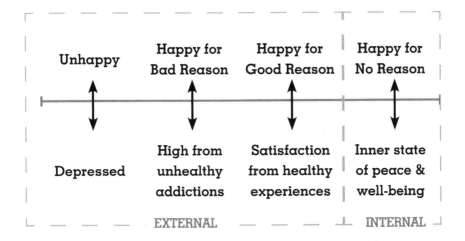

Unhappy: We all know what this means: life seems flat. Some of the signs are anxiety, fatigue, feeling blue or low—your "garden-variety" unhappiness. This isn't the same as clinical depression, which is characterized by deep despair and hopelessness that dramatically interferes with your ability to live a normal life, and for which professional help is absolutely necessary.

Happy for Bad Reason: When people are unhappy, they often try to make themselves feel better by indulging in addictions or behaviors that may feel good in the moment but are ultimately detrimental. They seek the highs that come from drugs, alcohol, excessive sex, "retail therapy," compulsive gambling, over-eating, and too much television-watching, to name a few. This kind of "happiness" is hardly happiness at all. It is only a temporary way to numb or escape our unhappiness through fleeting experiences of pleasure.

Happy for Good Reason: This is what people usually mean by happiness: having good relationships with our family and friends, success in our careers, financial security, a nice house or car, or using our talents and strengths well. It's the pleasure we derive from having the healthy things in our lives that we want.

31

Don't get me wrong. I'm all for this kind of happiness! It's just that it's only half the story. Being Happy for Good Reason depends on the external conditions of our lives—these conditions change or are lost, our happiness usually goes too. Relying solely on this type of happiness is where a lot of our fear is stemming from these days. We're afraid the things we think we need to be happy may be slipping from our grasp.

Deep inside, I think we all know that life isn't meant to be about getting by, numbing our pain, or having everything "under control." True happiness doesn't come from merely collecting an assortment of happy experiences. At our core, we know there's something more than this.

There is. It's the next level on the happiness continuum—Happy for No Reason.

Happy for No Reason: This is true happiness—a state of peace and well-being that isn't dependent on external circumstances.

Happy for No Reason isn't elation, euphoria, mood spikes, or peak experiences that don't last. It doesn't mean grinning like a fool 24/7 or experiencing a superficial high. Happy for No Reason isn't an emotion. In fact, when you are Happy for No Reason, you can have *any* emotion—including sadness, fear, anger, or hurt—but you still experience that underlying state of peace and well-being.

When you're Happy for No Reason, you *bring* happiness to your outer experiences rather than trying to *extract* happiness from them. You don't need to manipulate the world around you to try to make yourself happy. You live from happiness, rather than *for* happiness.

This is a revolutionary concept. Most of us focus on being Happy for Good Reason, stringing together as many happy experiences as we can, like beads in a necklace, to create a happy life. We have to spend a lot of time and energy trying to find just the right beads so we can have a "happy necklace."

Being Happy for No Reason, in our necklace analogy, is like having a happy string. No matter what beads we put on our necklace—good, bad, or indifferent—our inner experience, which is the string that runs through them all, is happy, and creates a happy life.

Happy for No Reason is a state that's been spoken of in virtually all spiritual and religious traditions throughout history. The concept is universal. In Buddhism, it is called causeless joy; in Christianity, the kingdom of Heaven within; and in Judaism it is called *ashrei*, an inner sense of holiness and health. In Islam it is called *falah*, happiness and well-being; and in Hinduism it is called *ananda*, or pure bliss. Some traditions refer to it as an enlightened or awakened state.

So how can you be Happy for No Reason?

Science is verifying the way. Researchers in the field of positive psychology have found that we each have a "happiness set-point," that determines our level of happiness. No matter what happens, whether it's something as exhilarating as winning the lottery or as challenging as a horrible accident, most people eventually return to their original happiness level. Like your weight set-point, which keeps the scale hovering around the same number, your happiness set-point will remain the same **unless you make a concerted effort to change it.** In the same way you'd crank up the thermostat to get comfortable on a chilly day, you actually have the power to reprogram your happiness set-point to a higher level of peace and well-being. The secret lies in practicing the habits of happiness.

Some books and programs will tell you that you can simply decide to be happy. They say just make up your mind to be happy—and you will be.

I don't agree.

You can't just decide to be happy, any more than you can decide to be fit or to be a great piano virtuoso and expect instant mastery. You can, however, decide to take the necessary steps, like exercising or taking piano lessons—and by practicing those skills, you can get in shape or give recitals. In the same way, you can become Happy for No Reason through practicing the habits of happy people.

All of your habitual thoughts and behaviors in the past have created specific neural pathways in the wiring in your brain, like grooves in a record. When we think or behave a certain way over and over, the neural pathway is strengthened and the groove becomes deeper—the way a well-traveled route through a field eventually becomes a clear-cut path. Unhappy people tend to have more negative neural pathways. This is why you can't just ignore the realities of your brain's wiring and *decide* to be happy! To raise your level of happiness, you have to create new grooves.

Scientists used to think that once a person reached adulthood, the brain was fairly well "set in stone" and there wasn't much you could do to change it. But new research is revealing exciting information about the brain's neuroplasticity: when you think, feel, and act in different ways, the brain changes and actually rewires itself. You aren't doomed to the same negative neural pathways for your whole life. Leading brain researcher Dr. Richard Davidson, of the University of Wisconsin says, "Based on what we know of the plasticity of the brain, we can think of things like happiness and compassion as skills that are no different from learning to play a musical instrument or tennis …. it is possible to train our brains to be happy."

While a few of the Happy 100 I interviewed were born happy, most of them learned to be happy by practicing habits that supported their happiness. That means wherever you are on the happiness continuum, it's entirely in your power to raise your happiness level.

In the course of my research, I uncovered 21 core happiness habits that anyone can use to become happier and stay that way. You can find all 21 happiness habits at www.HappyForNoReason.com.

Here are a few tips to get you started:

1. **Incline your mind toward joy.** Have you noticed that your mind tends to register the negative events in your life more than the positive? If you get ten compliments in a day and one criticism, what do you remember? For most people, it's the criticism. Scientists call this our "negativity bias"—our primitive survival wiring that causes us to pay more attention to the negative than the positive. To reverse this bias, get into the daily habit of consciously registering the positive around you: the sun on your skin, the taste of a favorite food, a smile or kind word from a co-worker or friend. Once you notice something positive, take a moment to savor it deeply and feel it; make it more than just a mental observation. Spend 20 seconds soaking up the happiness you feel.

2. **Let love lead.** One way to power up your heart's flow is by sending loving kindness to your friends and family, as well as strangers you pass on the street. Next time you're waiting for the elevator at work, stuck in a line at the store or caught up in traffic, send a silent wish to the people you see for their happiness, well-being, and health. Simply wishing others well switches on the "pump" in your own heart that generates love and creates a strong current of happiness.

3. **Lighten your load.** To make a habit of letting go of worries and negative thoughts, start by letting go on the physical level. Cultural anthropologist Angeles Arrien recommends giving or throwing away 27 items a day for nine days. This deceptively simple practice will help you break attachments that no longer serve you.

4. **Make your cells happy.** Your brain contains a veritable pharmacopeia of natural happiness-enhancing neurochemicals— endorphins, serotonin, oxytocin, and dopamine—just waiting to be released to every organ and cell in your body. The way that you eat, move, rest, and even your facial expression can shift the balance of your body's feel-good-chemicals, or "Joy Juice," in your favor. To dispense some extra Joy Juice—smile. Scientists have discovered that smiling decreases stress hormones and boosts happiness chemicals, which increase the body's T-cells, reduce pain, and enhance relaxation. You may not feel like it, but smiling—even artificially to begin with— starts the ball rolling and will turn into a real smile in short order.

5. **Hang with the happy.** We catch the emotions of those around us just like we catch their colds—it's called emotional contagion. So it's important to make wise choices about the company you keep. Create appropriate boundaries with emotional bullies and "happiness vampires" who suck the life out of you. Develop your happiness "dream team"—a mastermind or support group you meet with regularly to keep you steady on the path of raising your happiness.

"Happily ever after" isn't just for fairytales or for only the lucky few. Imagine experiencing inner peace and well-being as the backdrop for everything else in your life. When you're Happy for No Reason, it's not that your life always looks perfect—it's that, however it looks, you'll still be happy!

Branding
Small Business

RAYMOND AARON

Branding is an incredibly important tool for creating and building your business. Large companies have been benefiting from branding ever since people first started selling things to other people. Branding made those businesses big.

If you're a small business owner, you probably imagine that small companies are different and don't need branding as much as large companies do. Not true. The truth is small businesses need branding just as much, if not more, than large companies.

Perhaps you've thought about branding, but assumed you'd need millions of dollars to do it properly, or that branding is just the same thing as marketing. Nothing could be further from the truth.

Marketing is the engine of your company's success. Branding is the fuel in that engine.

In the old days, salespeople were a big part of the selling process. They recommended one product over another and laid out the reasons why it was better. Salespeople had credibility because they knew about all the products, and customers often took the advice they had to offer.

Today, consumers control the buying process. They shop in big box stores, super-sized supermarkets, and over the Internet—where there are no salespeople. Buyers now get online and gather information beforehand. They learn about all the products available and look to see if there really is any difference between them. Consumers also read reviews and check social media to see if both the company and the product are reputable. In other words, they want to know what the brand is all about.

The way of commerce used to be: "Nothing happens till something is sold." Today it's: "Nothing happens till something is branded!"

DEFINING A BRAND

A brand is a proper name that stands for something. It lives in the consumer's mind, has positive or negative characteristics, and invokes a feeling or an image. In short, it's a person's perception of a product or a company.

When all goes well, consumers associate the same characteristics with a brand that the company talks about in its advertising, public relations, marketing and sales materials. Of course, when a product doesn't live up to what the company says about it, the brand gets a bad reputation. On the other hand, if a product or service over-delivers on the promises made, the brand can become a superstar.

RECOGNIZING BRANDING AND ITS CHARACTERISTICS

Branding is the science and art of making something that isn't unique, unique. Branding in the marketplace is the same as branding on a ranch. On a ranch, ranchers use branding to differentiate their cattle from every other rancher's cattle (because all cattle look pretty much the same). In the marketplace, branding is what makes a product stand out in a crowd of similar products. The right branding gets you noticed, remembered, and sold—or perhaps I should say bought, because today it is all about buying, not selling.

There are four main characteristics of branding that make it an integral part of the marketing and purchasing process:

1. **Branding makes you trustworthy and known.** Branding makes a product more special than other products. With branding, a normal, everyday product has a personality, and a first and last name, and people know who you are.

   In today's marketplace, most products are, more or less, just like their competition. Toilet paper is toilet paper, milk is milk, and a grocery store by any other name is still a grocery store.

   However, branding takes a product and makes it unique. For example, high-quality drinking water is available from just about every tap in the

Western world and it's free, but people pay good money for it when it comes in a bottle. Branding takes bottled water and makes Evian.

Furthermore, every aspect of your brand gives potential customers a feeling or comfort level that they associate with you. The more powerful and positive that feeling is, the more easily and more frequently they will want to do business with you and, indeed, will do business with you.

2. **Branding differentiates you from others.** Strong branding makes you better than your competition, and makes your product name memorable and easy to remember. Even if your product is absolutely the same as every other product like it, branding makes it special. Branding makes it the first product a consumer thinks about when deciding to make a purchase.

    Branding also makes a product seem popular. Everyone knows about it, which implicitly says people like it. And, if people like it, it must be good.

3. **Branding makes you worth more money.** The stronger your branding is, the more likely people are willing to spend that little bit extra because they believe you, your product, your service, or your business are worth it. They may say they won't, but they will. They do it all the time.

    For example, a one-pound box of Godiva chocolates costs about $40; the same weight of Hershey's Kisses costs about $4. The quality of the chocolate isn't 10 times greater. The reason people buy Godiva is that the brand Godiva means "gift" whereas the brand Hershey means "snack." Gifts obviously cost more than snacks.

4. **Branding pre-sells your product.** In the buying age, people most often make the decision on which products to pick up before they walk into the store. The stronger the branding, the more likely people are to think

in terms of your product rather than the product category. For example, people are as likely, maybe even more likely, to add Hellmann's to the shopping list as they are to write down simply mayo. The same is true for soda, ketchup, and many other products with successful, strong branding.

Plus, as soon as a shopper gets to the shelf, branding can provide a quick reminder of what products to grab in a few ways:

- An icon or logo
- A specific color
- An audio icon

BRANDING IN A SMALL BUSINESS

Big companies spend millions of dollars on advertising, marketing, and public relations (PR) to build recognition of a new product name. They get their selling messages out to the public using television, radio, magazines, and the Internet. They can even throw money at damage control when necessary. The strategies for branding are the same in a small business, but the scale, costs, and a few of the tactics change.

Make your brand name work harder

The name of a small business can mean everything in terms of branding. Your brand name needs to work harder for your business than you do. It's the first thing a prospective customer sees, and it is how they will remember you. A brand name has to be memorable when spoken, and focused in its meaning. If the name doesn't represent what consumers believe about a product and the company that makes it, then that brand will fail.

In building your product's reputation and image, less is often significantly more. Make sure the name you choose immediately gives a sense of what you do.

Large corporations have millions of dollars to take a meaningless brand name and make it stand for something. Small businesses don't, so use words that really mean something. Strive for something interesting and be right on point. You don't need to be boring.

Plumbers, for example, would do well setting themselves apart with names like "The On-Time Plumber" or "24/7 Plumbing." The same is true for electricians, IT providers, or even marketing consultants. Plenty of other types of business are so general in nature they just don't work hard enough in a business or product name.

Even the playing field: The Net

The Internet has leveled the playing field for small businesses like nothing else. You can use the Internet in several ways to market your brand:

Website: Developing and maintaining a website is easier than ever. Anyone can find your business regardless of its size.

Social Media: Facebook, Instagram, LinkedIn, YouTube and Twitter can promote your brand in a cost-effective manner.

BUILDING YOUR BRAND WITH THE BRANDING LADDER

Even if you do everything perfectly the first time (and I don't know anyone who does), branding takes time. How much time isn't just up to you, but you can speed things along by understanding the different levels of branding, as well as the business and marketing strategies that can get you to the top.

Introducing the Branding Ladder

Moving through the levels of branding is like climbing a ladder to the top of the marketplace. The Branding Ladder has five distinct rungs, and unlike stairs, you can't take them two at a time. You have to take them in order, and some businesses spend more time on each rung than others.

You can also think of the Branding Ladder in terms of a scale from zero to 10. Everyone starts at zero. If you properly climb the ladder, you can end up at 12 out of 10. The Branding Ladder below shows a special rung at the top of the ladder that can take your business over the top. The following section explains the Branding Ladder and how your small business can move up it.

THE BRANDING LADDER	
Brand Advocacy	12/10
Brand Insistence	10/10
Brand Preference	3/10
Brand Awareness	1/10
Brand Absence	0/10

Rung 1: Living in the void. Your business, in fact every business, starts at the bottom rung, which is called brand absence, meaning you have no brand whatsoever except your own name. On a scale of one to 10, brand absence is,

of course, zero. That's the worst place to live and obviously the most difficult entrepreneurially. The good news is that the only way is up.

Ninety-seven percent of businesses live on this rung of the Branding Ladder. They earn far less than they want to earn, far less than they should earn, and far less than they would earn if they did exactly the same work under a real brand.

Rung 2: Achieving awareness. Brand awareness is a good first step up the ladder to the second rung. Actually, it's really good, especially because 97 percent of businesses never get there. You want people to be aware of you. When person A speaks to person B and says, "Have you heard of "The 24/7 Plumber?" You want the answer to be "yes."

On that scale of one to 10, however, brand awareness is only a one. It's better than nothing, but not that much better. Although people know of your brand, being aware doesn't mean that they are interested in buying it. Coca-Cola drinkers know about Pepsi, but they don't drink it.

Rung 3: Becoming the preferred brand. Getting to the third rung, brand preference, is definitely a real step up. This rung means that people prefer to use your product or service rather than that of your competition. They believe there is a real difference between you and others, and you're their first choice. This rung is a crucial branding stage for parity products, such as bottled water and breakfast cereals, not to mention plumbers, electricians, lawyers, and all the others. Brand preference is clearly better than brand awareness, but it's less than halfway up the ladder.

Car rental companies represent a perfect example of why brand preference may not be enough. When someone lands at an airport and needs to rent a car on the spot, he or she may go straight to the preferred rental counter. If that company has a car available, it's a sale. However, if all the cars for that company have been rented, the person will move to the next rental kiosk without much thought, because one rental car is just as good as another.

Exerting brand preference needs to be easy and convenient!

If all you have is brand preference, your business is on shaky ground and you can lose business for the feeblest of reasons. Very few people go to a second or third supermarket just to find their favorite brand of bottled water. Similarly, a shopper may prefer one store over another, but if both stores sell the same products, he or she will often go to the closest store even if it is not the better liked one. The reason for staying nearby does not need to be a dramatic one—the shopper may simply be tired, on a tight schedule, or not in the mood to travel.

Rung 4: Making it you and only you. When your customers are so committed to your product or service that they won't accept a substitute, you have reached the fourth rung of the Branding Ladder. All companies strive to reach this place, called brand insistence.

Brand insistence means that someone's experience with a product in terms of performance, durability, customer service, and image has been sufficiently exceptional. As a result, the product has earned an incredible level of loyalty. If the product isn't available where the customer is, he or she will literally not buy something else. Rather, the person will look for the preferred product elsewhere. Can you imagine what a fabulous place this is for a company to be? Brand insistence is the best of the best, the perfect 10 out of 10, the whole ball of wax.

Apple is a perfect example of brand insistence. Apple users don't just think, they know in their heads and hearts, that anything made by Apple is technologically-advanced, user-friendly, and just all-around superior.

Committed to everything Apple, Mac users won't even entertain the thought that a PC may have positive attributes.

Apple people love everything about their Macs, iPads, iPhones, the Mac stores, and all those apps. When the company introduces a new product, many of its brand-insistent fans actually wait in line overnight to be one of the first to have it. Steve Jobs is one of their idols.

Unfortunately, you can lose brand insistence much more quickly than you can achieve it. Brand-insistent customers have such high expectations that they can be disillusioned or disappointed by just one bad product experience. You also have to consistently reinforce the positives because insistence can fade over time. Even someone who has bought and re-bought a specific brand of car for the last 20 years can decide it's just time for a change. That's how fickle the world is.

At 10 out of 10, brand insistence may seem like the top rung of the ladder, but it's not. One rung is actually better, and it involves getting your brand-insistent customers to keep polishing your brand for you.

Rung 5: Getting customers to do the work for you. Brand advocacy is the highest rung on the ladder. It's better than 10 out of 10 because you have customers who are so happy with your product that they want everyone to know about it and use it. Think of them as uber-fans. Not only do they recommend you to friends and family, they also practically shout your praises from the rooftops, interrupt conversations among strangers to give their opinion, and tell everyone they meet how fantastic you are. Most companies can only aspire to this level of customer satisfaction. Apple is one of the few large corporations in recent history that has brand advocates all over the world.

Brand advocacy does the following five extraordinary things for your company.

Brand Advocacy

1. **Provides a level of visibility that you couldn't pay for if you tried.** Brand advocates are so enthusiastic they talk about you all the time and reach people in ways general media and public relations can't. You get great visibility because they make sure people actually listen.

2. **Delivers free advertising and public relations.** Companies love the extra super-positive messaging, all for free.

3. **Affords a level of credibility that literally can't be bought.** Brand advocates are more than just walking testimonials. They are living proof that you are the best.

4. **Provides pre-sold prospective customers.** Advocate recommendations carry so much weight that they are worth much more than plain referrals. They deliver customers ready and committed to purchasing your product or service.

5. **Increases profits exponentially.** Brand advocates are money-making machines for your business because they increase sales and decrease marketing costs.

For these reasons, brand advocacy is 12 out of 10!!

BRANDING YOURSELF: HOW TO DO SO IN FOUR EASY WAYS

If you're interested in branding your product or company, you may not be sure where to begin. The good news: I'm here to help.

You can brand in many ways, but here I pare it down to four ways to help you start:

1. **Branding by association.** This way involves hanging out with and being seen with people who are very much higher than you in your particular niche.

2. **Branding by achievement**. This way repurposes your previous achievements.

3. **Branding by testimonial.** This way makes use of the testimonials that you receive but have likely never used.

4. **Branding by WOW.** A WOW is the pleasantly unexpected, the equivalent of going the extra mile. The easiest and most certain way to WOW people is to tell them that you've written a book. To discover how you can write a book, go to www.BrandingSmallBusinessForDummies.com.

The Secret to Words

JACQUELINE LUCIEN

When you first learned to read, you probably were taught to associate each letter with an object and a sound. It was pretty flat-footed, like "A" is for apple or "B" is for ball. The things your parents or teachers used to illustrate the sound represented by each letter may have made sense to you? Did you ever wonder what the letters originally stood for, *or if they stood for anything* or how someone came up with their specific shapes and curves?

Each letter we use today has a rich and fascinating, multi-layered meaning. Each has a history of associations that make it just about perfect in terms of its shape and design. Just like Chinese and Japanese characters, each letter of the alphabet represents so much more than just a sound — it tells a story and conveys the ancient and original meaning in a powerful way which influences our words today. So, how did these letters that mean so much in our daily lives come to be in the first place?

We all know the old saying that a picture is worth a thousand words. Well, it's true and nowhere more so than when talking about the letters we use to read and write. The alphabet is connected to ancient pictures, and the essence of those pictures comes from both concrete objects and abstract ideas. If a picture is worth a thousand words, and letters (in their ancient essence) are pictures, *what is the worth of one letter? What is the worth of one word?*

THE CREATION OF THE ROMAN ALPHABET

The Roman alphabet (the 26 letters from A to Z used to create the English language) originated in Ancient Egypt. (The Romans influenced, and were influenced, by many cultures.) The Egyptian form of writing is called *"Mdu Ntr,"* Medu Neter or the hieroglyphics of KMT, *which means the Language of the Gods.* The characters, sometimes called ideographs, pictographs or phonograms, are symbols or pictures used to represent sounds or words. From these Ancient Egyptian hieroglyphs, letters were created. Each letter shape can be traced back to a hieroglyph, and the hieroglyph itself (or its meaning) can be directly connected to the way in which we use that letter on a daily basis.

How wonderful it would be for me to regale you with a story about the origin of each of our 26 Roman letters, but that would take a whole book — and that is something for another time. Instead, let's focus on the Roman letters A, B, D, and P, as well as the connection between the Gods and letters "G" and "N." The origins of these letters range from simple to complex, and provide a broad view of how the Roman alphabet came to be.

A IS FOR "APED/VULTURE

It is fairly safe to say that the letter "A" is one of, if not, the first letter children learn. As I mentioned, it is highly likely that a child first learns "A is for apple". What that child doesn't get taught is that "A" stands for lots of other things that actually better relate to the letter itself. After all, an A is a high reaching letter coming to a point; a round apple looks nothing like an A.

In ancient times, for example, a child might have been told "A is for aped." The Egyptian word "aped" is represented by a hieroglyph of a bird; and translates to the scientific word for bird (more specifically, vulture). The vulture ("aped") has a bad reputation these days, but was originally known for being a high-flying bird that valiantly cared for its young. The aped was also considered the Pharaoh's favorite bird. Clearly, the aped had a high station in the culture, making it a great choice for the first letter of the alphabet.

Digging deeper, let's look at the qualities represented by the letter A itself, and how those qualities are related to the aped. The A is reminiscent of pyramids; it is a triangle with great heights. Further, the aped is linked to words like "Air"... "Altitude"... "Ascend" ... "Appreciate" — words that all have meanings connected to greatness, height and direction. These words' meanings, coupled with the fact that the letter A is represented by a distinct and greatly appreciated bird, are all indicators of why the capital letter A itself is visually tall and reminiscent of height.

There is a second 'glyph' represented by an arm, thus the word arm. And, for example, it is the "a" in leverage. Thus, one would have to make a distinction between which glyph is represented in the word in question. This will be elaborated further in my book, along with many other examples.

Further, the great Egyptian God Amun, an incredibly influential and powerful God, is later called "Amen," the same word used by many religions to end a prayer. The importance of the A is so great that it is used, in part, to finalize the hopes and thoughts of multitudes of people to ensure that they are heard and responded to by their equivalent of the great Egyptian God Amun. Jumping ahead, Amun is an ascended / high and wise/seeing god.

B IS FOR BARE FOOT

In continuing with our exploration into letter origins, let's look at the letter "B". It originates from the hieroglyph of a bare foot. Among the first qualities we can associate with a bare foot is down (or downward) as the bare foot is at the bottom, or base, of the body. (Can you see a pattern emerging?) The bare foot is support for the body, like a brace or the base of a table. The bare foot helps with movement, bringing you to where you need to be. "Bottom"... "Base"... "Brace"... "Bring"... These words indicate support in both stillness and movement.

The letter B itself is sturdy. The bottom, larger than the top, stabilizes the letter, holding the letter upright, just as the bare foot holds up the rest of the body. When we look at the shape of the lowercase "b," we see its appearance is very similar to that of a leg and barefoot. Other examples of how the letter shows up in our language include: "Boots on the ground" and "Battalion," both representing foot soldiers.

D IS FOR DIGITS /HAND

The letter "D" originated from the hieroglyphic symbol of a hand. The Egyptian word for hand is drrt , The function of the hand (because of our opposable thumbs) separates man from the animals. Man does many things with his hand(s). Among the words that start with D, and are connected to the hieroglyph, is the word "digits," i.e., the fingers of the hand. Digits help man "Do" things… "Duty"… "Drive"… "Diligence." These words are all connected to man doing and accomplishing something. Even more closely linked to the letter D and the hieroglyph of the hand are words such as "dexterous" and "dexterity." The meanings of these words are directly related to hands and the ability of the hand to perform tasks. Thus, D has the quality of action and is directly related to the action of the hand. *Even though the English word hand does not start with the letter d its meaning is consistent in the word.*

⬜ P IS FOR PORTAL/DOOR

You may be wondering why I chose to jump all the way to "P" at this point. It's because of the very interesting connection between two letters that I want to share with you. The Egyptian hieroglyph for "P" is a square, more specifically, a door. Now, think about the letter D again. If you were to turn the lowercase letter "d" around (by 180 degrees), what would you have? Yes! A small letter "p"! The d in the picture of the door that we see in the hieroglyph is truly a p, as in the word "Portal." I also looked across languages in Spanish you have puerta.

While it might not be your first thought, when considering doors or portals, we are truly thinking of going out into an open space or a place that affords opportunity (opportunity having the double-p, or two portals… even the word "port" is embedded in "opportunity"). The letter P is instrumental in many common sayings, including, "When opportunity knocks, answer the door" and "window of opportunity." These sayings allude to the double-p (two portals) in opportunity, and the door or portal at which to respond to the opportunity being given to you. So the quality of a door to be considered is that it is an opening, something you can go through. The words that come to mind are: passage...privilege...progress....port....peer (as in look through).

THE LETTERS OF THE GODS

A deeper analysis of letters and hieroglyphs reveals the remarkable way in which some letters correlate with the ancient Gods worshipped by the Egyptians. To appreciate the connection between the two you need to know a bit about Egyptian Cosmology.

Cosmology in general is the study of origins and the universe. Egyptian cosmology revolves around the required balance between humans and the Gods. Humans believed that if they were cooperative, kind and just to one another, the Gods would, in turn, be kind and keep the forces of nature in balance. There are many Gods in Egyptian Cosmology: The God of the ground/earth (Geb), the God of the night/sky (Goddess Nut), the God of the sun (Re), the God of air (Shu) and the God of chaos (Nu). I'm going to focus on the first two Gods, Geb and Nut, for the next part of our journey through the alphabet.

G IS FOR "GEB

The letter "G" comes from the hieroglyphic letter or symbol for the stool. In this respect, the stool is defined as a stand upon which you put a jar. That definition suggests support, foundation, and a most telling word, "grounding" (the stool is on the ground). The "G" also represents the Egyptian God, Geb. As previously mentioned, Geb is the God of earth itself. Egyptian cosmology states that Geb is quite literally the earth... the "ground"... the "geography"... the "globe". The earth "gives" and supports life. The earth "grows; "it generates." As a result, it makes perfect sense for the letter "G" to come out of a symbol that represents an object that grounds and supports, and is the foundation for other objects and beings. Geb is also shown supporting or holding up Nut, the night/sky. Geb is Nut's husband/brother. Does that give you something to consider regarding the ancient wisdom for the need to support?

N IS FOR NUT
∧∧∧∧

The letter "N" originated from the hieroglyph of wavy lines, similar to waves and water. Some say that N represents water, which is a source of life. Also, similar to the letter G, the Roman letter N is connected to both Egyptian hieroglyphs and the Egyptian Gods.

In Egyptian Cosmology, there is the Goddess Nut. She gave birth to the sun, and the sun revolves around her body in a 24-hour cycle to make night and day. Nut is commonly depicted as a woman who is arched over the earth (Geb) on hands and feet. The Goddess Nut is representative of the barrier between chaos and the cosmos and is seen as a protector of the dead whom she keeps with her in her starry sky.

The Goddess Nut is the night, the darkness from which everything derives. In English, she is the "Night". In Spanish, she is the "Noche"... in French "Nuit"... in Greek "Nyx" ... Nacht in German ... "Nox" in Latin ... in Sanskrit "Naktam" and in Hindi "Nishaa."

"Nyx" (Ancient Greek: **Νυξ**, "night")" in the Latin translation is the Greek goddess, or personification, of the night. A shadowy figure, Nyx stood at or near the beginning of creation and was the mother of other personified Gods such as Hypnos (Sleep) and Thánatos (Death). Nyx's appearances in mythology are few and far between, but what has been revealed about her is that she is a figure of exceptional power and beauty. Nyx is found in the shadows of the world and is only ever seen in glimpses. As you get away from the source, the object or concept can gain other interpretations.

When we see the reference to Nut as protector of death, it represents that, as time went on, words that were powerful from the opposite quality. The words that come to mind are English "no" ... Spanish "nada," ...german "nicht", " nein"

I urge you to continue with your own exploration of the word "night", its spellings and meanings across languages. It is unlikely that the Gods from one belief system to the next can be so similar in both names and existence without it being anything less than purposeful.

So… what does all of this Goddess Nut and Night talk have to do with the Roman letter N? Well, the letter N is derived directly from Nut. And, again, Nut is the night, a bringer of life (like the water depicted in the hieroglyph), and the protector of the dead. Nut's role is natural and nurturing. Nut is the N in origin, beginning, expansive and garden. She is the N in neuter, as she was disempowered through time and forgotten for her role as giving birth to the son. And, what about the word "not" representing further neutralization and negation? As you look at how she is depicted, with her arching body, you can see she is the N in expansive beginning and origin. She is also the N in the words span and extend over or across something, like space and time.

The capital letter N looks physically similar to the waves in the hieroglyph.

Interestingly, the depiction of Nut in her arched form is also similar in shape to the lowercase Roman "n". These connections between Roman letters, hieroglyphs, and Ancient Egyptian Gods cannot be ignored or thrown aside. These connections are very much real.

Ok, I Can See It. But Why Should I Care?

While reading thus far, have you said to yourself, "this may be interesting, but how can I use this information?" Or, are you thinking that this chapter satisfies a little curiosity, but that's it; you'll move on to something else because this information does not have any real purpose for you. How can you actually use this in your life?

Doesn't this understanding of letters make them seem so much more alive? Have you not gained a greater appreciation for the letters we use to construct our most meaningful of words? Consider for just a moment how much more enlightening the learning of the Roman alphabet could be to a five-year-old child if he or she were taught by way of hieroglyphics, meaning and origin. The very nature of learning would be greatly enhanced.

Children would not only learn what each hieroglyphic and Roman letter looks like, but would also understand their meanings. Learning the origin of each letter provides the opportunity to more fully grasp the how and why of each shape and sound, as well as the connection of these shapes and sounds to the bigger piece – reading words as a whole. Further, understanding each letter's origin enhances the learning of vocabulary and spelling by making connections with the meaning of letters and the purpose each holds within a word. The more we use our five senses to learn, the more mastery we can have. *Children could be encouraged to put letters together to create their own words, another form of creativity and another way to tell their story. I invite you to consider additional uses for this information.*

BUT I'M BEYOND LEARNING TO READ

Pictures provide a very profound way to anchor learning and memory. Further, pictures and words, particularly when they work together, are exceptionally useful tools for drawing you in to a subject. Graphic artists are taught to come up with abstract ideas and create logos to convey meaning, (the same thought process used to create the hieroglyphics) while advertisers use words and pictures to gain access to your mind and influence your perception.

As an example, let's talk about the soda 7UP®. Would the brand name affect you the same way if it were 7b? (The b that is downward and associated with the bare foot.) No, of course it wouldn't, because, in its essence, 7b is a "downer." So, instead, we are sold 7UP, which includes the letter P associated with an upward door, an opening and an *opportunity* for something. The brand name 7UP is pure genius. Without the understanding and purpose of our letters, we are unable to understand the cause and effect of what we are seeing.

Also, by unlocking the meaning of letters, you can cross check the dictionary or encyclopedia and go beyond the history of the words, the etymology to understand how letters and words interact with each other. What are the letters really saying? Why is it that a word can mean something in one language, but mean something completely different in another language? When you explore the reference tools I just mentioned, you see that the meaning of a word changes according to the culture and powers that be at the time. Now you have the tools to see how the story of the letters supports the dictionary meaning, or not, and why.

Learning occurs in stages; since this is an introduction I chose words to represent the concepts presented, primarily having the letter at the beginning of the word. Once there is a command of the concept you begin to see its function in any part of the word.

Further, we can empower children by providing them with an understanding of the meanings and origins of the letters in their names. We can challenge them to personify each letter and gain strength, courage and leadership skills based on the history associated with their names. The big picture impact is that we can teach children to read and write with this new perspective. We can use the origin and meaning of letters to create logos and company names that are more powerful and impactful than ever before. We can provide another efficient way to remember names by seeing what the letters in the name say. We can advance into the future by using the keys provided by our world's ancient history and earliest writing.

If you would like more information about hieroglyphics in general, or want to learn more about the meaning of a specific letter or word, like your name, please feel free to contact me at jahkey2@gmail.com .

Project Management

How to be Extremely Efficient and Remain Profitable While Developing Any Project

GUSTAVO A. VALENZUELA

The Project Management Institute (PMI) officially defines project management as the application of knowledge, skills, tools and techniques to project activities to meet the project requirements.

To properly manage any project, you must have acquired, through actual management experience, specific knowledge pertinent to the needs of the project. Furthermore, as a project manager, you must have skills in negotiation, decision making, trust building, crisis management, conflict management and verbal and oral communication. These skills and more are needed to remain in control of the entire project's team and their performance. However, being able to visualize and fully understand the project as a whole is probably the best ability you can have and is necessary in order to know immediately, at any phase and at any given time, if the project is moving forward in the best possible way.

LOPPM (LACK OF PROPER PROJECT MANAGEMENT)

In many situations, project owners without a project manager can only appreciate the services of a seasoned project manager when the project is in crisis and they are desperately seeking help. This is not an unusual situation, as people will often take on projects without fully understanding what they are getting into. They'll sign the contract, then get slammed by the intricacies of the project. and the many requirements and processes they must follow, without realizing that an experienced project manager is the ideal person capable of delivering the project within scope, schedule and budget.

While working closely with project owners, I concentrate on increasing their involvement in the entire project development. As a result, they're thrilled to feel in control of their project, especially their budget. They truly appreciate having my experience and expert advice as I act as their project manager. If you would like to benefit from the services of an experienced project manager, please visit www.TheBookonPM.com

WHO RUNS PROJECT MANAGEMENT?

You, as the hired project manager, are responsible for running all such entities, while also keeping in mind that stakeholders may influence your process, something that deserves to be seen as an opportunity for you to remain in control of managing the project—as long as you hold them accountable and make them aware that budget, project schedule and scope may be affected by their requests and attempts to run your project.

WHAT IS AND WHAT IS NOT PROJECT MANAGEMENT?

Initially, your main goal is to select the most effective and ideal team that will run itself without micro or macro managing every aspect and assigned task. If you're successful and your budget can afford to assemble a team of experts, the project will most likely run smoothly (as long as you're able to properly manage it). Having the best team doesn't mean you can stop acting as the project manager. You must also watch all aspects and processes; the scope, compliance, the budget and the schedule. Allowing things to happen and disconnecting your management eye from a project because you've established trust and confidence in the team's abilities isn't really considered project management.

Even when you have the best team to develop your project, a successful project manager is always looking for opportunities to improve the process, to save money, to be more efficient and perhaps even to discover new ways to improve the bottom line. There are opportunities with every project to adjust, improve and even systemize processes to become more efficient, to stay engaged throughout the entire process and to capitalize on those opportunities. By performing your duties as a project manager at all times, your expertise and level of confidence will be elevated and will rightfully separate you from amateur project managers seeking to complete a project just as required.

When you ask yourself "What is Project Management?" you may now add, "The ability to remain connected and engaged throughout the entire process in order to positively affect scope, budget and schedule."

A ROBUST DEFINITION FOR PROJECT MANAGEMENT

As you work in project management, you'll realize the importance of taking your duty as a project manager beyond your contractual agreement. You are already expected to apply your knowledge, your skills and your techniques to meet the project requirements. But by choice, you must make it a personal practice to consciously look for the greatest benefit for the project regardless of what is in your project manager contract.

Project management is inclusive of moral values for both personnel and stakeholders, project managers must also have proper understanding while managing diverse personalities, cultural differences and beliefs. Your decision to go beyond management of project scope, budget, schedule, risk, quality and resources sets you apart from the herd.

How will you know when you are going the extra mile? When you come to that situation in which you tell yourself "This is outside my contractual duties," but you're certain that if properly addressed and handled it will positively influence the outcome of the project—and you simply choose to do it.

To download guidelines on effective steps and ideas on how you may push yourself to consistently go the extra mile, please visit www.TheBookonPM.com

Last, in a new definition of project management, you could easily add,

"The ability to include everything tied to any project and place it under the responsibility of a qualified project manager who's able to handle whatever arises, always taking action for the benefit of the project." That would be an all-inclusive contract only a few project managers would confidently sign. If you include yourself in that list of the selected few that would sign such a contract, you are a project manager at heart.

WHY PROJECT MANAGEMENT?

Anyone with the financial means to do so can develop an intent to manage a project without the proper knowledge and specific experience. However, the results will not be favorable for any of the variables that matter, such as scope, budget and schedule. The truth is they will lose money—in the millions—as a result of their innocence and obvious unsophistication in the subject. In the United States, around 68% of the projects fail in at least one of the three critical areas and 98% of those failed projects lacked the services of a project manager. Even more revealing, the remaining 32% of the projects that did not fail were properly organized and managed by an experienced workforce and included the services of an experienced project manager. More so, for every billion invested in the United States, $122 million is wasted due to lack of project performance and proper management. Even more shocking, the failure rate is 50% higher for projects with budgets over $1 million. In most cases, the project owner doesn't even know they are losing money or that they are overspending.

Next time you are acting as a project sponsor or if you are the actual project owner, realize that you may not have the correct talent in your organization to properly develop a project. Additionally, make the right choice and wisely avoid assigning your project and its management to an inexperienced workforce.

EFFECTS OF HAVING AN EXPERIENCED PROJECT MANAGER

The simplest way of saying this is that having an experienced project manager in your development team managing every aspect of your project is the equivalent of having a cardiovascular surgeon perform open heart surgery on you rather than the Chief Executive Officer (CEO) of the hospital. Only project managers can do the job of a project manager, despite the common belief that anybody in the team can wear multiple hats and perform several duties. The effects of having an experienced project manager will indeed be favorable and noticeable, always revolving around success.

LOSING CONTROL AND MONEY

The margin for keeping or losing control of your project is very narrow. There are a number of factors that can be directly related to losing control of your project. Scope creep, departing staff, wrong skill sets being allocated to the project ad lack of focus from the project team can all lead to disaster and you losing control of the project.

Managing tasks, keeping an open communication line with your active team members and setting the stage for upcoming team members are all good practices for staying in control. Many outside factors may also cause you to lose control of the project and if that is the case, your immediate attention is required. Take a step back and reassess the situation as a whole. Once you've gained complete understanding and a clear picture, you may develop a plan to begin turning the project around and back on track. As soon as you identify and begin to tackle a challenge, you have begun gaining control of the project.

Losing money in a project is often tied to key pieces of information being excluded or overpriced by vendors and which are crucial for a successful project completion. You must also have a well-developed ability to review and negotiate bids, quotes or any costs associated with the project. Hence, it is vital that a project manager has the project owner first review the entire project scope and then approve all proposed costs for the correct and just amount of money. Project owners tend to ignore these critical initial operations. At the end, this translates to loss of revenue via wasteful unnecessary spending to the point that your project is not fully completed or ready for occupancy.

To download guidelines and a checklist on effective steps you may take to avoid or stop losing control and money, please visit www.TheBookonPM.com

ACCOUNTABILITY OF STAKEHOLDERS

As a project manager, you're required and expected to execute processes and move through project phases in a clear way so that the planning and approving process for scope is definitive and formal, as to avoid and minimize changes. Hence, when any stakeholder—including the project owner or sponsor—requests a change in scope, budget or schedule you can hold them accountable for what they've requested. People, in general, change their minds constantly and if you're one of those project managers who make challenging and impossible projects seem easy because of your expertise, organizational skills and outstanding people skills, owners will feel invited to propose changes anytime they feel like it. There's a lot at stake and it's your duty to communicate and paint a clear picture for all stakeholders. Formally and officially remind the project owner about the process for approval of scope then pull out and present their approval document with their signed name, signature and date. Point out the paragraph addressing "changes in scope" in which, in sum, it communicates that after approval, and especially during the middle of production, any changes in scope will drastically and most definitely affect budget and schedule. If the owner is still adamant about his request, prepare the correct documents and amend the project's budget to properly compensate your team for accommodating such a late request.

HOW MANY PHASES ARE FOUND IN PROJECT MANAGEMENT?

As a project manager you'll go through the basic phases in any of the projects you're managing. These phases may include: initiating, planning, execution/ production, monitoring/controlling and closing or close out phase. These are the general overall main phases or, in simple terms, the summary of the whole picture.

As a project manager, it is advantageous if you choose to see subphases within major phases. A phase is simply a grouped set of goals or requirements containing a number of steps. Once completed in the allocated time, that phase has been attained and the project can progress to the next phase. So, it's for your own benefit, as you become an extraordinary project manager, to identify what those subphases are in your project.

By breaking down a phase into subphases or a major set of goals into individual goals, you have created a daily, weekly or monthly to-do list to execute your job as an effective project manager. Moving from goal to goal or from point A to point B has new meaning. This simple technique will allow you to visualize and understand the whole picture of any project and at the same time, it will allow you to see and understand the smallest detail of the project.

WHEN TO ENGAGE A PROJECT MANAGER

As a project owner or sponsor, as soon as you get an idea to develop a project, call a project manager and hire him to assist and represent you in the entire process. Nonetheless, at any phase of the project a seasoned project manager can keep things clear, honest and legal. A project manager can hold everybody accountable and in strict compliance with their contractual obligations, on behalf of the project owner and in consideration of established goals of the project. The earlier a project manager is engaged, the more beneficial it is for stakeholders and the project variables, including scope, budget and schedule.

To hire and benefit from having the expert advice of a project manager in your organization, please visit www.TheBookonPM.com

EFFICIENCY DEFINITION THROUGH A PROJECT MANAGER'S LENS

Improving your abilities and skills to manage scope, time, quality, costs and risks logically and habitually happens after you completely understand projects as a whole and after having the benefit of actually managing several projects from start to end and beyond

Only when choosing to know all the project details and team requirements is efficiency born. Then you as the project manager acting as a project leader and working closely with stakeholders can define critical project milestones. Having open communication allows you as the project manager to attain pertinent documentation required to easily move the project forward. Equally as important, understanding and managing risks on a daily basis and taking corrective action will drastically improve overall efficiency.

HOW TO GET AN "A-TEAM"

The success of your project is based in great part on the quality of experience of your selected team members. Therefore, during team selection, first seek for relevant, proven and verifiable experience that is as close as possible to the requirements of your project type. Second, look for people with strong abilities to solve problems and verify they have the right knowledge and access to tools to tackle the most complex challenges the project may face. Third, evaluate their longevity and stability in the specific tasks they're working on. Last, ask them to enlist their strengths and explain why they're interested in becoming part of your team. Always check the validity of all information as submitted and do verify their references.

After accomplishing full compliance with the project's legal requirements, you may assist the procurement team with verifying the project's technical and special requirements. Intentionally choose a diverse selection committee with specific expertise in different areas of the development, including scope, execution, finance, policy, technical, maintenance, warranty, life cycle, or other areas identified as important to the specifics of the project.

Once you have performed all these duties, you ought to consider receiving from all vendors a formal statement or summary of qualifications (SOQ) as part of the documenting process. Gather, review and rank all information, and then interview the top five vendors.

To download a smart list of SOQ items, please visit www.TheBookonPM.com

THE RIGHT INTERVIEW QUESTIONS

Efficient project management is directly related to efficient use of time and opportunities. Utilize the interview to ask only questions that will give you a new insight into the vendor's knowledge, expertise or specific skills. Also, use the interview time to ask the tough questions vendors are not usually asked.

When submitting a written SOQ, the vendor has all the time in the world to formulate a written answer. However, during an interview the vendor only has seconds or minutes to formulate and give his response. As a result, his response is real and it informs you how this particular vendor will handle things during the development process. It's easy for a vendor to state in writing that they have years of experience and can handle your project, but during the interview, if you formulate real questions based on actual project requirements, you'll be able to tell if that vendor is truly knowledgeable and has the right procedures and tools to move the project forward.

Ask questions about all critical areas of the process, including, initiation, planning, execution, monitoring and controlling, closing out, warranty, operational phase and sustainability. This line of questioning truly filters vendors. Those with real, honest experience are able and willing to share their answers in great detail. Then, verify their response by calling their references.

To rely on the expert advice of a project manager to guide your team during vendor interviews, please visit www.TheBookonPM.com

EFFICIENT WAYS TO GET YOUR PROJECT DONE

After you wisely organize processes and all project tasks are properly delegated, you must concentrate on maximally producing or realizing tasks on that specific day; Verify that critical tasks' requirements are clearly identified, that the required work for execution has been delegated to the right party. Then verify the project is performed as planned. Always be two steps or more ahead of your own schedule. Before, during and even after project development, continuously ask yourself "How can I be more efficient?" Any and all ideas that come to mind, simply try them out. If they're successful, choose to make them part of your process on all your future projects.

ORGANIZATION BASED ON EFFICIENCY AND FLOW

The number of people and tasks required to properly and successfully complete a complex project is immense. Subsequently, intending to keep track of them all in your mind is not an efficient way to get your project done. A single organizational chart depicting names, assigned tasks (below stakeholder's titles) and properly organized by the project's phases allows for an efficient way to channel information for proper review and approval. Indeed, an entire project's directory is an important document to keep updated for the benefit of effective project management. Relying on a complete organizational chart is a clear way to see the entire picture, including the review and approval process for each of the project phases.

Organizational charts with detailed information regarding the review and approval process can show the flow of important information either up or down. Up information may include items such as change order requests, payment application requests or allowance use authorizations. Down flow information may include an instance when an owner requested a change in scope, a failed inspection report or a corrective action plan. If an owner sees graphically, in an organizational chart, how many people he's affecting with his "simple request to change scope" he or she may reconsider his request.

Use a detailed organizational chart as a tool for stakeholders to realize the importance of understand positioning and flow in the project's team. As a result, this will create continuity and efficiency.

RECOGNIZE THE ACTUAL STATUS OF YOUR PROJECT

As you create your progress summary report, make a commitment to be completely honest as you report on scope, budget, timeline, risks, quality and percentage completed. Sometimes owners get feedback from other sources and honesty will be your best practice if it comes down to verifying the validity of your report. Reporting on all areas of the project helps your efficiency and saves time as you avoid having several separate meetings.

If the project risk is high on any project area, formulate potential solutions on how to mitigate or eliminate such risks. Any solutions you present ideally you've already discussed with your team prior to presenting them to the project owner. It's important to report on key areas without inundating stakeholders with too much information, especially if it is technical information.

Staying in control of the project also allows stakeholders to sense and see that the project is in great hands and that you are on top of things and two steps ahead.

MONOTONY = BORED DISCONNECTED TEAM

It's true that repetition makes you better at anything, however, during project development, a lack of variety and interest paired with a tedious routine may affect the moral and emotional well-being of your team. Anytime you have a team who is bored working on your project, you're close to having a team that is disconnected from your project. After disconnect comes inefficiency and inevitable mistakes or inaccuracy with scope compliance.

There are many ways you can avoid monotony or promote variability. One way is to allow your team members to fully understand the project's mission and not just the task at hand. You may choose to reward an early finish and accuracy as a way to keep the team excited about accelerating their portion of the work and being accurate and in full compliance with scope.

You may also share some exciting news about the project such as plans to submit for a worldwide recognition award or being acknowledged on important social media sites as a way to recognize them for their portion of the work. The main idea is to avoid monotony and make your team feel appreciated. You want to periodically remind them that their portion of the project is just as important and meaningful as the rest.

For other great ideas on how to keep your team motivated, please visit www.TheBookonPM.com and download a complete list of ideas and techniques, which will keep your team energized and connected to your project.

SYSTEMIZING THE PROCESS

Ideally, your system model wisely accommodates individual expression. This means that as long as the team's creative choices during execution yield the established and required system results, team members can decide how and in what ways their execution may be more fun, efficient and varied. The goal of having a system is to create organization and improve predictability. Furthermore, a system allows for new team members to enter the system and become productive in the least amount of time possible.

Having expert skills and knowledge in a particular field drastically increases your accuracy when completing a specialized task. For instance, you may recognize that your expertise in project management is what gives value to your daily work and your brand. Likewise, recognizing your team's individual expertise will allow you to properly delegate tasks and increase accuracy to the point of achieving perfection.

ELEMENTS OF A GREAT SCHEDULE

A schedule is basically WHAT needs to done, by WHEN and WHO is responsible for it. The project schedule is also required to comply with contractual milestones and it must be formulated with the level of detail required by the contract.

Schedules can serve as a daily, weekly and monthly guide and they're a reliable tool to verify estimated versus actual progress for the completed portion of the project. The level of detail or task description in a schedule varies depending on whom the schedule is written for and what the true intent is for having it.

You may also consider adding enough information to allow listed tasks to act like a to-do list. In fact, including critical reviews and approvals and listing an inspector's information may be extremely practical and beneficial. Adding the sequence for review and approval and listing appointed personnel to perform such duties will be a great way to organize and make the entire team aware of critical inspection events.

Note: Every time you catch yourself thinking "I need to remind myself to do this," and that specific task is not on the schedule, simply add it and test if having such information listed is beneficial to the entire team.

LOOK FURTHER INTO CRITICAL TASKS

Is it possible to dig deeper into critical tasks and find information worth sharing on the project schedule? Absolutely! If you further investigate and understand who is at the bottom of any task or performing any type of work, including review or approval, then adding their information to the schedule will provide you with another level of management. Make a practice to identify every single person involved in any of the processes. By doing so, you'll be able to expedite compliance with that specific task.

FACTORS SHAPING YOUR SCHEDULE

There are other factors shaping or affecting a project's schedule and knowing these factors exist helps the team to plan and allocate time just in case they arrive. Although some of these factors impacting your project schedule, such as climate and accidents, are completely outside your control, you may still formulate a plan to mitigate their effects on your schedule. In the case of climate, knowing climate trends and identifying rainy seasons can help you plan for such an event.

Other factors difficult to plan or accommodate in your schedule include sick people, new hires, new trends, changes in scope, additional safety, omissions, new regulations, unforeseen conditions, etc. You, as the project manager working with your team, may formulate and agree on a plan of action to take if any of the previous factors happen to arrive during your project. Having an agreed plan of attack drastically reduces downtime and excuses for not having a potential solution in place.

HOW TO ADDRESS UNFORESEEN CONDITIONS

In every project, unforeseen conditions and events arrive and test your skills and ability to find solutions. There are some basic steps you must take in order to address unforeseen conditions. First, immediately attend to it by identifying who's in charge of that specific portion of the project. Secondly, once you identify the appropriate party, perform an internal "911" or urgent phone call to the individual in charge to explain the emergency and the urgency for them to address the issue at hand immediately. Third, look at your schedule for float and identify items you may borrow time from to address the unforeseen condition. Then take necessary measures to resolve the issue effectively. Last, choose to plan ahead of time for unforeseen conditions by creating an allowance in your budget for such situations. One of the main reasons unforeseen conditions do not get immediately attended is because there are no funds allocated to pay for the required resources to solve the matter at hand.

Follow the steps listed above on every project you manage and you'll certainly handle any unforeseen condition as a true professional in charge of managing the entire project development.

To benefit from the expert advice of a project manager, to receive assistance reviewing your project's documents or to identify potential unforeseen conditions prior to officially starting your project, please visit www.TheBookonPM.com

WHAT CREATES UNWANTED CHALLENGES IN A PROJECT

Unwanted challenges are often created by unrealistic owner expectations with scope, budget or schedule. Also, inadequate project funding and an inexperienced owner or stakeholder making critical project decisions will always result in an undesirable turn of events. It's common to invite unwanted challenges as early as when procuring and selecting a team if selection is solely based on costs instead of experience or expertise. Even as you review and approve their contracts, having insufficient contractual responsibilities will invite your team and project to face unwanted challenges. As a project manager, the inability to exercise stakeholder accountability may also bring unnecessary, challenging situations to the project. Once unwanted challenges arrive, the project may enter into crisis.

THE CRISIS MANAGER

If you're ever invited to handle a project in crisis, it's a clear sign that you've gained the respect and trust from the project owner, a sponsor or your employer. If you're a great, experienced project manager, you probably have gained the respect and trust from all three entities already. Project managers who can see the big picture and understand every phase and every single detail of the complete development of a project can in fact and will certainly jump on the opportunity to take over a project in crisis. It's like a doctor performing surgery on a patient diagnosed as inoperable or incurable. The doctor goes in with all he's got and does what he does best and cures a patient deemed incurable.

Once assigned to handle a project in crisis you must assume the responsibility of solving any and all project issues and challenges without assigning blame. It's the professional and right thing to do. Let attorneys do their job, when their services are engaged. Managing a project in crisis is about finding solutions and implementing the best solutions to gain control of the project and by having a clear mission to get it back on track. Your immediate goal ought to be to do whatever it takes to guide it and manage it to a successful completion.

When you act as a crisis manager it's a perfect opportunity to display your knowledge, expertise and acquired specialized management abilities. If, on the other hand, you're a project owner or a sponsor, keep in mind that one sure way to get your entire team and your project into a crisis is to choose to develop a project without the services of an experienced project manager.

AM I TO SAVE, FIX OR PULL THE PLUG?

There are instances in which the only option is to terminate a project. The most obvious reason is when financial resources have been exhausted and there's no money to save, fix or complete a project. Also, anytime a project is affecting and endangering public safety, you must consider ending such a project. The main reason project management takes place is precisely so that the project gets completed. Salvaged projects brought to completion help stakeholders and they also help you become a better project manager. Therefore, work to rescue a project before you come to the conclusion to terminate it. Your final recommendation to stakeholders must be a professionally written statement listing your precise reasons for why the project is to be salvaged or terminated.

DEFINITION OF A SUCCESSFUL PROJECT

Is a pleased project owner enough of a reason to consider the project a success? Of course, it's not. If you hit the targets defined in your scope and the project is in absolute compliance with your budget and schedule, then you may correctly state that you have completed a successful project.

Relying on successful values, such as honesty, confidence, perseverance, integrity, innovation and adaptability, provides a solid base for success to rest upon. Celebrating your victories and embracing your challenges helps you learn and become better. These are also crucial factors to be included in your ever-changing formula for success.

Write your own definition of success and share it with the rest of the project's team. It will provide a clear target and allow for recognition and celebration when the team hits the bull's eye and the project's purpose is accomplished. Watch for the team and stakeholders saying "WOW" and use that as an indicator that success is surely on its way.

To create "WOW" experiences on all your projects, and to learn how the proper management techniques will create the "wow" factor everywhere, please visit www. TheBookonPM.com

PROJECT DELIVERY WITH A MISSION

Knowing the specific purpose for developing a project allows project management to revolve around a clear mission. A project manager who's aware of the main project's mission and understands the "What," "Why," and "Who" can easily focus resources around these reasons.

Make it part of your own personal practice to ask the project owner or sponsor, why this project? And do ask about the mission or main purpose for developing this project.

PROJECT MANAGEMENT BENEFITS YOUR BUSINESS PROFITABILITY

Learning to delegate responsibilities is an ability you develop once you fully comprehend, through extensive experience, what people can do for you and the project. Project managers are experts in understanding what each team member is responsible for and what each is capable of contributing to the progress and completion of the project.

Inexperienced project owners tend to delegate tasks to the inappropriate person or party. For example, they ask engineers questions meant for architects and ask architects to attend issues meant for a general contractor. During project management, simple mistakes cost money—a lot of money.

Money allows the project to start, then project management allows the project to move forward and, last, it allows for the completion of the project. It's a fact that money is truly the heart of the project and without it, the project may not survive. As you become more efficient and knowledgeable about reviewing and approving costs, your ability to reduce overspending by millions of dollars will increase. It will also allow your project management skills to benefit any organization financially.

To increase your business's bottom line and maximize profit, please visit www. TheBookonPM.com and schedule a professional consultation with an experienced project manager.

EVERY PROJECT IS UNIQUELY DIFFERENT

Even if you work in franchise project development and every project has the exact same requirements and goals, so they all look the same, the simple fact that the project is in a different location will make that project uniquely different. It's true, no two projects are alike, and as you recognize that every project has a unique set of rules and variables you'll begin to adapt to properly managing the differences in your projects.

Project management expands across several industries and is a profession practiced worldwide. Since scope for projects are diverse, procurement and team members are also diverse. It's like a meal using the exact same ingredients but cooked by different chefs; the taste and even the way the meal is served on the plate will be different. Subsequently, it's a smart practice to systemize your processes used during the project development to become more efficient and to allow repetition of tasks, so the parts of your process become automatic and predictable. In a way, the variables and differences in a project are what makes project management enjoyable. And, truthfully, your ability to handle the differences in diverse projects is what makes you a unique project manager.

A MEASURING STICK

How do you measure your project's success? There are many indicators to tell you that your project is going well and that you're being successful. For instance, a happy owner who's recommending you to other clients to the point that he already sold your services is a great sign that you're on the right track. Perhaps success shows up as passing every inspection with flying colors and earning the respect of inspectors. But for many people who trade their talent and time for money, the ultimate indicator for success comes via a significant bonus at the end of the year. You may have all or some of the previously mentioned indicators, but other important factors may not be present, such as the emotional well-being of the entire team. Moreover, there may be vendors who feel they were strategically obligated to do things outside their contract just to gain the opportunity to do business in future projects.

When half of the indicators aren't present and you receive an award, how would you feel about being recognized? On the other hand, if all indicators are there and no award is given, you'll probably feel blissful and accomplished.

It's nearly impossible to measure the true success of a project. You can't expect everybody to be completely satisfied, fully pleased and always preferring you as their project manager. Having stated this, how about outlining, during the planning process and scope definition, what would be considered a success for the project you're managing? This may give you a clear target that's easy to identify and a set of guidelines and expectations regarding the positive outcome of the project. Ask for and document a definition for success for your project in your detailed scope, vision, mission or your "goals documents." Then, work to get there.

CLOSE OUT

It's time to finalize all project activities and verify everything is completed across all phases. As you enter this phase and close the project to transfer the completed project as required the end of the road for the majority of your team members is near. You, as the project manager, have some critical and important steps to take before you sign off on the closing of all phases. During this phase it's critical to involve all project participants and stakeholders and use a robust checklist to make sure you cover each and every item that has been completed.

Soliciting feedback as you conduct a post-project survey is more opportunity to understand how the entire team feels about the project as a whole and in specific areas outlined in your survey. Including a "lessons learned" meeting allows you to gather useful information for the benefit and success of future projects. During this phase the collecting of project data to be archived is the actual deadline for the majority of the team members. If your project requires archives to comply with any regulations such as NARA (US National Archives and Records Administration) or others, verify that all submitted documents and data are in full compliance.

The checklist pertaining to your close out procedure may be extensive as every project has its own unique requirements and stakeholders often require specific information, such as financial audits. They may also have confidentiality requirements and may require disposal of sensitive information in order to properly close out a project. Ideally, your checklist for the close out phase is amended with every project you manage and it's your practice to always include a formal meeting with stakeholders prior to arriving at this particular phase.

USEFUL LIFE COSTS

For many developments, project management ends at the completion of a project, once the owner takes full control of the completed product. Infrequently, the project manager participates in managing the warranty period, typically lasting up to two years. Depending on the project delivery method, you may be asked to remain in the project since you are the official holder of the information pertaining to just about everything regarding the completed project.

If you're given the opportunity to participate in the management of a completed project, such as a building, while occupied by its end users you will get to see its operations and experience the maintenance phase. Thus, your ability to see the whole picture and have a better watchful eye during production will get sharper—since you'll have important knowledge about why things fail and need to be repaired during the two-year occupancy period (in the case of a building).

Always make the owner aware of the importance of performing a life cycle cost analysis, which simply means a complete understanding of total costs of ownership. Having the financial means to develop a project until the point of making it functional and operational is considered by most a healthy project budget. Eventually, the daily operational costs requirements of the building begin along with its demands for repairs and replacements. Often keeping up with expenses becomes such a big challenge that businesses are closed, buildings are abandoned or their functionality is limited.

To benefit from the services of an experienced project manager, please visit www. TheBookonPM.com and schedule a professional consultation.

SUSTAINABILITY

How long can anything be maintained at a certain rate or level? Even more specific, how long can a project sustain its healthy life while serving its intended function? And last, for how many years can it be sustained without undesirably impacting its surroundings or the environment?

The UN World Commission on Environment and Development definition for sustainability reads: "Sustainable development is development that meets the needs of the present without compromising the ability of future generations to meet their own needs." Now, since buildings require money to stay alive, let's look at financial sustainability. Imagine two people are sitting side by side and each of them have one dollar. The only way these two people may remain side-by-side is to give a dollar and then receive a dollar. So person "A" gives a dollar to person "B" at the same time person "B" gives a dollar to person "A" This process, as long as it happens precisely as described, can be sustained indefinitely. When there are multiple streams of income, including sophisticated systems for income generation coupled with a sound administration for all finances, your odds for remaining sustainable just increased.

Every project is to include the commonly avoided sustainability conversation since many project owners usually ignore it. Carefully bring this subject up and address its requirements. Working closely with all stakeholders, do your best to utilize the entire team's abilities. If you must, hire expert advice.

DECODE, DECRYPT AND DECIPHER

Documenting the entire process and creating a reliable system to access it, read it and understand it, may be one of the major challenges the project development industry faces. The information produced before, during and after a project in development is vast as it's inclusive of everything in relation to the entire life cycle of that project.

The main purpose for documenting a project is to have the ability to understand how, what, who, when and why things were developed in a certain way. There are many processes to organize, archive and access information, however no software out in the market does it all. Hence, you may be required to provide a hybrid solution to comply with project archiving and retrieval.

Make it a practice to document project information in a clear way so that 30 years from today, anybody who accesses the project database will be able to fully understand it.

A FINAL NOTE

Now, give yourself credit. Your project management knowledge, skills and tools have been complemented just by the mere fact you have read this book. Your journey as a project manager will be filled with amazing opportunities to leave this world a better place. Your participation in project management along with millions of fellow project managers around the globe will add to the efforts of the fastest growing profession in the world. Be efficient, honest and stay true to your values. Surprise yourself first, and every project you manage will become successful in every way, just as you imagined it. Share your story; spread the joy and your knowledge to those around you. You're already an amazing project manager. All that's left to do is for you to let it come out.

It is time to play! Enjoy your journey, as you may now efficiently and profitably perform project management.

The Mindset of Success

ANNA GRIFFIN

My mother said something to me once that has stuck in my mind ever since, and that is, "Conviction and comfort don't live in the same block." If you want your life to be fulfilling and continually reach your goals and dreams, then there are going to be times of discomfort and overcoming fear.

When I started writing this chapter, I was completely filled with fear, uncertainty, and confusion. I guess it was fear of having my thoughts heard, and thinking, "Who am I to say all this?" or "What will others say?" These types of thoughts and questions often accompany us in moments when we least want it or expect it. "Am I strong enough?" "Am I going to be accepted and will I fit in?" are our common thoughts. But quickly enough I thought to myself, "Well, what's the worst thing that is going to happen?" I set myself back on track to have the right mindset and to think of the many exceptional leaders I have been fortunate to work for throughout my career and travels.

I've made it my mission to understand their exceptional attributes, which served them in moments of fear and self-doubt. But it is not always about the tools that are being used, the business models or the frameworks. Often, it is more about their mindset and leadership and what kind of people we become in their presence.

Living in many countries and getting to know different cultures, from the West to the East, I have had the privilege to better understand what makes a person successful, happy, and someone you would want to follow as a business leader, or because of their humble yet inspiring way of life.

So, I searched, and continue to search, for inspiration from them and the application of their mindsets, their extreme discipline, and their right habits in real life and workplace. The understanding of how we can be enemies to ourselves when it comes to fulfillment and achieving what we really desire in life prompted me to share and get it all out. Not only that, it was a true journey into myself that gave me clarity about what will come next.

In my book, Reimagine the Possible, I go into details of the attributes and tools of success and happiness, and how to apply them to your life. In this chapter, I am going to highlight some of them, to get you started on your road of possibilities.

THE WILL TO CHANGE

"It isn't the mountain ahead to climb that wears you down.
It's the pebbles in your shoes."
- Muhammad Ali

There are a few distinct features that set successful people apart from those who fail. It's not always the talent or number of titles they have behind their name, but it's their mindset and the few things they do differently than majority of us. First, they are able to develop strong and fulfilling relationships, alliances, and connections that will help them build their business, create their success, and open the doors to potential opportunities.

Second, they don't procrastinate, but act on their plan, and the things they passionately want to do. Often, what most people do is wait until the perfect time comes and put things off till tomorrow that they should do today; e.g. "I'll start my new online business when I get more support from my partner or the economy is better," or "I will create a better website for my business once my kids get out of the house." "I will start taking care of myself later." There is always a 'but' that we keep saying to ourselves.

Third, they don't give up, they are persistent, and they keep going with their plan. They understand that success will not be achieved instantaneously. How often do we start something but never finish it because it gets too tough, too time-consuming, or too overwhelming? If we face those few things and persevere, I believe, we might be quite successful and happy in our professional and personal lives.

Of course, the journey is never easy. Success doesn't happen overnight. It will take time, but if you believe in your abilities, have the right mindset and perseverance, and above all work hard, you will get there. The hard work is not only related to achieving your professional or career goals. It is also hard work on yourself, your beliefs, fears, and habits, all of which this chapter will discuss.

What's important is not what you will or will not do, or whether you will or will not change. It is whether you have the will to change – to plan and act so that you can start doing the things that you know you should.

NO SMOOTH MOUNTAIN

We keep dreaming about how one day we could reach our full potential, and the goals we always wanted to get to. But we often don't realize that we are as capable of genius as the most successful people in the world. We look at people like Oprah, Steve Jobs, and Richard Branson, and think, "If I only had their ideas, their genius", or "They are so lucky." You ask yourself, "How can I find my true purpose and passion in life? Why can't I never figure out how to be successful and happy like them?" But nobody, and especially the most successful in the world, thinks they are special until they make themselves special.

Nobody starts their business knowing that they will instantly become multi-billionaires. The difference starts with their mindset, the plan they have, and the actions they take. What sets the successful people apart from the less successful ones is that they do what most people don't want to do or are hesitant to do. Perhaps they hesitate because they are terrified of the unknown or they believe they are too busy, that it's beyond their capabilities, or maybe people around them would say it's not possible, that it is out of their reach and they will never get there. The other group, the fulfilled ones, listen to themselves and pursue their dreams, no matter the obstacles, and they ignore the naysayers.

Will you struggle? Will it be hard? Yes. You may fall many times, but who is counting? The best successes are made from failures. In fact, I don't believe there are failures, only lessons learned. You must remember that no single mountain is smooth. If you want to get to the top, there are sharp ridges that must be stepped over. There will be times that will be stressful, and you might be disappointed and discouraged.

FEAR

"No person can be confronted with a difficulty which has not the strength to meet and subdue. Every difficulty can be overcome if rightly dealt with. Anxiety is, therefore, unnecessary. The task which cannot be overcome ceases to be a difficulty and becomes impossibility and there's only one way of dealing with an impossibility, namely to submit to it."
- Byways of Blessedness, James Allen

When we are confronted with difficulties, over time they create a great amount of anxiety. We may be faced with decisions that have long-term ramifications for our life or career and would affect not only us, but also those close to us. Those are decisions that we would rather not have to make. They just make us want to pull a blanket over our head and wish they would disappear together with the light that disappears once the same blanket covers our hair.

93

The question that I started to ask myself was, "Where are my fears coming from and why am I allowing them to stop me from moving forward?

James Allen's words in the quote are very profound, and the essence is that there is no problem that cannot be resolved. I like to think about it in this way: if an issue that I am facing can be resolved with an action, then I don't have an issue. It is simply something that needs to be resolved and is just something that we encounter in our lives or at work. So, remember, if an issue can be solved with action, then it is not an issue.

This has been my approach to any challenge that has been placed in front of me throughout my career and life. I treat it like something exciting to resolve and put my best effort into coming up with the best solution.

A substantial body of research shows that our brain can't actually differentiate physical fear (e.g. car crash) from emotional fear (e.g. being afraid of a spider). In addition, research also shows that in the brain fear and excitement are caused by the same neurochemical signals, i.e. cortisol and norepinephrine. Steven Kotler talks about this at length in his research, and shows that fear and flow (or the peak performance) are at the opposite sides of the same spectrum. They are both caused by the same neurochemical reaction in the brain, initiated by cortisol and norepinephrine.

Successful people learn to reframe the fear and use it as their compass; if something that they want to do produces some level of fear, then this is exactly what they will do. They will do what scares them the most, what feels uncomfortable. Only by doing this will they be able to push their boundaries, and this will give them the progress and growth needed to accomplish what they want. Below are some ways that help to acknowledge and reframe fear:

1. Acknowledge the changes that are happening and how they are affecting you – how does the event make you feel?

2. Ask 'Do I have enough information and facts to support my fear?'

3. Reframe the context. Say to yourself that you are excited about the event. This will switch your brain from feeling anxious and nervous to feeling excited and positive (no danger is coming).

4. What's the payoff? What is the price that I will pay if I don't reframe and stay in the state of fear, which will negatively impact my performance and future prospects? What will my career look like?

You must remember that we fear and are anxious about things that we create in our minds and imagine that they may happen to us. We think that external forces create our anxiety or fear and we only respond to those events. But our response to any situation, however bad it may be, is our choice and the result of our thoughts and beliefs.

I always like to remind myself that most things that we imagine out of fear never happen. Mark Twain famously once said, "I have lived a long life and had many fears, most of which never happened."

MASTER THE MINDSET

"Beliefs have the power to create and power to destroy," as Tony Robbins, the motivational speaker and life coach, said. You see, our beliefs about the events around us or what happens to us are what shaped us into who we are today and who we will become tomorrow. But the fact is that many of us grew up around people who inadvertently passed on their limiting beliefs to us, and we might have been conditioned to the negative thinking that they grew up with. But remember, our past doesn't define us and there is no point in playing the blame game with them for passing their limiting beliefs onto you.

Research tells us that our thoughts and responses are shaped by our subconscious mind and they are aligned to the paradigms that we grew up with. For example, you might have had people in your life who constantly told you, "Since you haven't done it till now, you are just not cut out for it." This environment conditioned your thoughts and created paradigms in your subconscious mind. You start creating excuses without even realizing it, and eventually you will quit pursuing your dream.

If you want to have a successful career or follow your dreams, you need to evaluate whether your own mind is your biggest enemy and if you are acting according to old paradigms that shaped your thoughts, and hence your decisions, actions, and results. If so, a change is needed.

First, you will need to decide that you want to change your paradigm. Change is never easy, but once you realize that some of your old patterns, actions, and decisions are a result of the environment you were raised in or are surrounded by now, then you will see how this impacts your current life. I always like to remind myself of something that Wayne Dyer, American philosopher and author, said: "When you change the way you look at things, things that you look at change." Don't make yourself a victim of the circumstances surrounding you, or those that you cannot control.

Our life, career, and relationships are a reflection of the approach we take towards them. We are fully responsible for how things turn out for us – whether we are successful or not, have savings, a fulfilled relationship at home, a loving family, and so on. Let's say, your team is not producing the results you wish, or your business is not going well. Perhaps you are not paying attention to the relationships within your team and let them just run, or maybe the decisions you made were not the right ones. We are the only ones that have the power to take responsibility for the change we are looking for. We waste our most finite resource, time, to find external reasons that cause change. But once we shift this mindset, our life, career, and relationships will start getting into gear.

So, whatever we've learned and experienced in the past, we've accepted it as a truth at an unconscious level, and now it doesn't matter if what we've learned is correct or not, we still accept it as a truth. These are the 'life's apps' that we created for each aspect of our life – you have an app for everything that gives you a point of reference to go back to and check out how it should be done. I've realized over the years how this led to developing unconscious behaviors and habits in me.

"The beliefs that you have about yourself and your abilities are not facts. They are your tightly held opinions. In other words, it's not primarily about your ability. It's what you believe about your ability that shapes your potential success."
- Dr. Stan Beecham, Elite Minds

I also realized how often my belief system was empowering me or, unfortunately, disempowering me. You can take any experience in your life and make it into a very meaningful and empowering capability. Or it can be the opposite; your experiences and beliefs can be limiting you. You can take a painful experience and make it into powerful and motivating strength that will empower you to do anything you dreamt of.

There are a few simple ways that can help you work on your old paradigm and create change. I have done this myself, and it helped me realize how my own old conditioning was affecting my life, career, and relationships.

- Ask yourself: What are the same behaviors and actions that cause the same results and do not allow you to move forward?

- Think about successful people: What are the behaviors and actions they would take to get the results they want?

- Write down and focus on the new habits and actions that you want, and consciously think about them when you catch yourself doing the old ones.

- Change your 'I can't' or 'I should' to 'I must' and 'I will.'

DON'T DRIFT...DISCIPLINE

For any muscle on our body to grow, it needs to be exercised and maintained continuously. The same holds the true for everything we want to accomplish at work or in life. If you want to be accomplished in anything, you need to get disciplined in doing things that matter, that are important, to bring you closer to success and set you on the path to whatever you want to do in life.

Of course, there are times when we need to take a balanced approach, but discipline for me is really an intrinsic quality that we all should strive for. It comes from within and starts with you. Oftentimes, we are looking for all sorts of shortcuts – the new meditation technique that will set us free, the new set of motivational tools, and the new supplement to get our body fit. But these may (or may not) work for a week, a month or 3 months, and if it's not coming from within us, it won't last. We don't do hard things if we are not emotionally attached to them.

If you look at leaders you admire, or the most successful people, you will see the level of discipline they have in their lives, and in doing things that set them apart from others, things that others are not willing to commit to. It is an intrinsic self-discipline – a matter of 'personal will' as Jocko Willink, a retired navy SEAL officer, calls it. The difference between being good and being exceptional is how disciplined you are.

He continues by saying, "Those who are at work before everyone else are considered best operators." But that discipline cascades down to everything else they do. Willink rightly said, in his book Extreme Ownership, that discipline equals freedom. This is very true – once you are disciplined with the things that you know you should be doing, it sets you free to do other things that you claimed not having time for, but which were in fact just an excuse, with the blame pointed everywhere else but at yourself.

OWNERSHIP

One of the most important things I have learned, that really impacts how successful you will become, is to take full ownership of the results that you produce, the challenges, everything that impacts your results, or even your personal or social life. If I didn't own the results that were expected of me or my team to deliver, I would have never achieved the level and quality that I wanted. I always expect the highest results, but that can only be done if I completely own it. It is an attitude, and the fundamental block of any success. Blaming others or making excusing not only doesn't help but it actually hurts the team, the company, and ultimately you. In some cases, we don't want to even acknowledge the problem, or are afraid to accept that we made a mistake because we don't want to take ownership of the consequences. This will not serve the team or help it win.

Mistakes happen in the workplace, especially with complex problems, diverse teams, and tight deadlines. We should be able to acknowledge it, come up with better solutions for next time, or reach out to others for advice. We have much more respect for a person who takes full responsibility for their actions and results, don't we?

When we look at the great leaders and successful people around us, we wonder how they make the right decisions in stressful situations, or remain calm when faced with chaos and complexity. But what sets them apart in such situations is that they carefully choose how they respond. They don't jump to a conclusion and decide out of an emotional outbreak. This is a critical skill if you aspire to be a great leader and to be successful.

Often, what we do is react to situations without thinking, and we don't choose our behaviors but just act them out. We respond in the way our mind is wired and how we were conditioned. This may sometimes have catastrophic results in the workplace or in our personal lives.

Victor Frankl, the Austrian neurologist and psychiatrist, and a survivor of concentration camp, wrote a fascinating book "Man's Search for Meaning", in which he describes his horrific journey through Nazi concentration camps between 1942 and 1945, where he moved four times between different camps, including Auschwitz, while his family perished. Frankl said, "Between stimulus and response there is a space. In that space is our power to choose our response. In our response lies our growth and our freedom." This is a very profound thought that can guide us to make a shift in how we react and respond.

The best leaders and successful people train themselves and practice various scenarios for responding rather than reacting to the situation:

1. Think about consequences and bigger picture – What will you achieve by reacting in specific way (e.g. in anger)? Will the response and consequences be aligned with your goals or plans? How will the response best serve you, your family, or your project and company?

2. Realize whether you are responding or reacting – This is important, because it will give you clarity if you are reacting out of anger, a lack of control, sadness, jealousy or perfectionism. If you pause and think about the root cause of your answer or reaction, you will be able to respond in a wiser, more thoughtful way.

3. Don't react out of emotions – This relates to the point above, but you will also need to realize that your best response is based on facts.

4. Realize that you have a choice and different options – When you are faced with a situation where you want to rush to react and respond harshly, realize that you have a choice, and consider the consequences of your reaction. Count to three, if you must.

HABITS

"What we know from lab studies is that it's never too late to break a habit. Habits are malleable throughout your entire life. But we also know that the best way to change a habit is to understand its structure — that once you tell people about the cue and the reward and you force them to recognize what those factors are in a behavior, it becomes much, much easier to change."
– Charles Duhigg 'Power of Habit'

A study was done by Wendy Wood, a Provost Professor of Psychology and Business at University of Southern California, on a group of people that was given stale popcorn in the cinema in exchange for rating a move. Most of the people ate the stale popcorn despite the fact that they said after the movie that they didn't like it. It turned out that they ate it out of their habit of being in the cinema. But what this shows us is that we often do things without realizing it and a, "Thoughtful intentional mind is easily derailed, and people tend to fall back on habitual behaviors," said Wood.

From the time you get up in the morning until you go to bed – most of what you do in between is without thinking; it's automatic. I mention automatic because it is a very important feature of habits, because we don't even realize what we are doing and why we do it. In fact, 40% to 45% of our daily activities is habitual, according to Professor Wood.

Everything we do or want to do is a step towards accomplishing a goal or achieving something that we desire – that goal might be to get to work, to satisfy hunger, to relax, to feel wanted, to get a promotion, and so on. Professor Wood explains that, "We find patterns of behavior that allow us to reach our goals. We repeat what works, and when actions are repeated in a stable context, we form associations between cues and responses."

It turns out that our brain creates patterns of activities, thinking, and behaviors that we do constantly and become automatic, so it doesn't have to spend energy to think about it each time (a simple example would be how to walk or brush your teeth). Our brain developed habits, so it doesn't have to think about them repeatedly and can have the space to focus on doing what's more important, like new projects at work, creating new product, writing, studying, making decisions, and more.

When we behave out of habit, our mental activity and alertness drops in the middle of it. Research shows that once we develop a habit and do something on autopilot, our brain is almost inactive, and so is our decision capability related to that activity. For example, when you are driving to work, you don't think, "Ok, now I need to decide to indicate that I want to turn right," do you? You don't make these decisions any more. When you were driving to work for the first time, you perhaps needed to think about which street to turn right onto. Over time, it became automatic.

Habits are developed slowly, and it is very hard for us to change the habit without completely knowing what the cues of that habit are. We must learn how to identify which cues led to a particular behavior, called cue awareness, so that we are at least aware and know when the habit is actually happening. Oftentimes, with certain strong behaviors, we don't realize the cue and, hence, we do them automatically. For example, some people bite their nails without realizing it, and they may now understand what the cue is (i.e. why they are doing it).

Have you found yourself with any habit that you do without understanding why, and you only realize it once you've done it? The important part of a change is to do it slowly through first recognizing when we have the urge or need to do the habit.

All successful people understand the importance of small improvements, which underpin our progress and have a profound impact on the long-term improvement. Imagine if you made just one tiny improvement every day. That small change, done every day, will turn into a habit and it will become part of your subconscious.

In the Japanese culture, this is called kaizen, which literally means 'improvement' or 'change for better,' and is fundamental to their professional lives and personal relationships. But the Japanese also understand that to see the change, we need to commit to it. Very often, what happens is that we set a goal, such as something that we want to improve. We might get excited and motivated at first, but that commitment fades after a few weeks and we forget to keep up our commitment. This comes back to understanding the triggers and wanting to change.

The single most important thing is our full commitment and then acting upon it. Without it, we will return to your original state in days. We really must be disciplined. At the end of the day, the most successful athletes didn't achieve their gold medals without true discipline. Yes, we will have obstacles, bad days, and days where we just can't do it anymore, but remember, after winter comes spring and summer. Don't think your winter will last forever.

Start small. Don't overwhelm yourself with too many things that you think you should, or want to, improve. It will only confuse you and you won't be able to achieve anything. To change your behavior long-term, you will need to:

1. increase your performance little by little every day, and

2. change your environment to get rid of the distractions that may keep you close to your old habits and behavior.

"We are what we repeatedly do.
Excellence, then, is not an act, but a habit."
- Aristotle

GROWTH AND FAILURE

There are no happy accidents that turn people into experts or that give people some special gift which allows them to live a happy and successful life.

We are not born into it. While some could be genetic, most of it is not. When we are born, our potential is unknown. We can accomplish whatever we can possibly imagine, and our abilities can be developed.

When we read about successful people or observe those around us who seem to have more success than us, be it better jobs, better relationships, or better health, what they all actually have in common is their constant hunger for growth and development. They never stop learning new things and upskilling themselves, their mind is always curious, and they want to push the boundaries of what is possible. All these characteristics underpin their growth mindset, which is critical to their progression.

"When you are in a fixed mindset, your success is a result of that belief. And all you will try to do throughout your life is to prove yourself against that fixed standard. In a growth mindset, challenges are exciting rather than threatening. So, rather than thinking, "Oh, I'm going to reveal my weaknesses," you say, "Wow, here is a chance to grow."
- Dr. Carol Dweck

Growth mindset is a scientific theory suggesting that with effort, persistence, and hard work, our intelligence and abilities can be developed. Dr. Carol Dweck, a psychology professor for Stanford University, showed through over twenty years of study of human development and psychology that our belief system about our abilities and potential fuel our behavior and predict our success. Dr. Dweck's early research was focused on how kids respond to failure, and shows how some children reacted positively to failures and setbacks, taking them as opportunities to develop, while others were completely devastated by them. Those kids who thrived on challenges adopted a growth mindset. They believed that with hard work, good strategies, and perseverance, they would eventually develop more skills and talents. Those who wanted to stay away from failure at all costs were in the fixed mindset.

"It's not how good you are. It's how good you want to be."
- Paul Arden

Very often, we see people who have very fixed beliefs about their abilities, what can be done or achieved, and what they can accomplish in their career or in life. For example, you hear at work, "This cannot be possibly done," or "It's beyond my capabilities." Perhaps we may see that in ourselves at times. We may think, "I'm not good at this," instead of "What am I missing?"; "This is too hard," instead of "This may take some time and effort,"; or "I'm obviously not good at finance," instead of "I'm not good at finance yet and keep studying."

People who don't progress through their lives or career only see obstacles that prevent them from achieving what they want, or what is achievable at all. They look at their abilities, skills, and performance, or even their health, fitness, and relationships as fixed and accept them as they are. This "fixed mindset," as Dr. Dweck describes, "makes us believe that our character, intelligence, and creative ability are static and cannot change or improve in any meaningful way."

You may see multiple examples of a fixed mindset around you. There might have been several projects or initiatives that were believed to not be achievable or were too hard to implement, and hence were abandoned. A project manager believed that the timeline was too short; there were no right skills or resources within the team; no right leadership or systems to support it; and the reasons why not could go on forever. Focusing on issues rather than solutions, and the things that would prevent the team from being successful would, indeed, bring no results.

With the right mindset and approach, even hard tasks can be achieved, issues can be resolved, and step by step, you will take the team closer to success. Remember that if an issue can be resolved with actionable tasks, you actually don't have an issue. This requires the right mindset to be in place, one that will see unlimited potential and the bending of the boundaries of what's possible.

This is what successful people do. If we look at the people whose success we admire, then we will see that they cultivate their growth mindset to enable their personal, professional, and social development and progression. Research shows that one of the reasons why we feel unhappy or frustrated in our jobs or personal lives is that we stop growing and progressing. We, as humans, are "designed" to evolve, and progress and growth is necessary to our wellbeing.

"If you imagine less, you will be what you undoubtedly deserve."
- Debbie Millman

With the growth mindset, as Dr. Dweck explains, we treat any setback as an integral part of our development and path to success. I have felt bad, embarrassed, or fearful of my mistakes and setbacks, but I've learnt that they would only help me to grow. Often, I came out on the short end with my decisions, but every time I aimed to tweak my approach to do better next time.

Growth mindset keeps our mind sharp. In today's work environment, we need to keep up with new technological and organizational developments. Things are changing and won't slow down anytime soon. To be ahead, we need to constantly learn.

Sometimes we find ourselves in moments where our fixed mindset kicks in, but the important thing is to realize it, snap out of that, consider more appropriate approach and move forward. Through "deliberate practice" we can change it – we must be purposeful and systematic about what we want to change. What helps me shift when I find myself in a fixed state are the four simple steps outlined below. They require a focused attention, and once you go through them, you will realize how destroying and limiting your fixed mindset can be, and instead will focus on developing more of a growth one.

1. Be aware that you are exposed to limiting thoughts based on your past and learn to be aware of your fixed mindset thoughts. What I mean by that is that we are prone to reject new opportunities, not because we are not able to do it, but because we are afraid of the unknown. Our brain is wired to search past experiences and do only what is known and in our comfort zone. Remember that this is only your brain's response to the unknown. It wants to keep you safe and it doesn't like risks and any unpredictability.

2. Acknowledge that you have the choice. We all have a choice about how we react and respond to any situation. How you interpret challenges, setbacks, and criticism is your choice. Whether you apply a fixed or growth mindset, it will have a chain reaction in what will happen next.

3. Replace fixed mindset talk with a growth mindset voice. Personally, I have had many moments when I dealt with self-doubt and feared to take on new challenging projects, was simply procrastinating, or too

lazy to do something. We have all been there. Over the years, though, I have learned to replace those damaging thoughts of a fixed mindset with the empowering thoughts and beliefs for growth. When I doubted myself and thought, "Can I do this? This is certainly not for me. I don't have the talent to do this," I immediately replaced those thoughts with empowering thoughts, such as, "I am certain I can do this and I will learn along the way," "I have passion and perseverance to accomplish this."

4. Take action that focuses on growth. Without action, there is no progress. Without facing the challenges and new opportunities, you will never learn. You must wholeheartedly commit to the challenge and overcoming any setbacks that will come your way. Learn from it and adjust as necessary.

FAILURES ARE YOUR GIFT

It is no secret that our worst fear is a fear of failure. However, failure is actually a good thing. It is just an opportunity to begin again, learn from it, and to do it more wisely next time. Encouraging our fears and failures prompts the most necessary changes in our lives and businesses. This may be true, but we don't often feel or think like that.

When we make mistakes, we feel terrible and disappointed; we lose confidence, and get discouraged. We just don't want to continue or go through it again. What we are actually doing is missing out on the primary benefit of failure. Winston Churchill once said, "Success is the ability to go from one failure to another without losing your enthusiasm." The man was right.

When it comes to failures, our egos are our own worst enemies. When something is going wrong, we try to save face and our defence mechanisms kick in, and we often find ourselves in denial. It seems very hard for us to admit and to try to learn from failure, because it requires us to challenge our status quo.

"I haven't failed. I have just found 10,000 ways that won't work."
- Thomas Edison

Look at Walt Disney, who was fired from the local newspaper he worked for because he was told he had no imagination. What his story teaches us is that just because you encounter a setback or end up on another path, it doesn't mean that you are stuck. Keep learning from your mistakes, apply changes to make things better, and you will get back on track eventually, and most likely, you will be better off than before.

There are many successful people who we can mention here who have failed but never gave up, e.g. Steve Jobs, Oprah, JK Rowling. What separates successful people from those who are unsuccessful is that they have a huge amount of perseverance. They never give up or let their failures define them. They pick themselves up even stronger than before and keep going. It's not always easy to continue moving forward, but when you keep pushing onwards, despite the failures and obstacles along the way, you are already ahead of all those people that just gave up. I find that the secret really is to just show up and try your best over and over again.

Failures are part of the process. To be successful, you must learn how to make it a tool rather than a roadblock. You must be adaptable and agile. When you stop learning from your mistakes, then you will stop growing and developing. You should take any failure as motivation in pursuit of your dreams. Don't let it stop you but grow you instead. The only failure there can be is when you quit. Learn the lessons, apply them, and you will come out stronger than before. You will never learn faster than you will by executing something.

NOTHING HAPPENS WITHOUT ACTION

Remember, talk is cheap! Action is everything. Our thoughts are catalysts to get started. But our thoughts are not things, and nothing will happen without taking those thoughts and putting them into action mode. That's what successful people focus on. They know that talking, planning, and analysing won't get them too far. It's their actions that will trigger all the things on their road to success. To be successful in any part of your life, you must be action-oriented. Mark Twain said, "The secret to getting ahead is getting started." You can't do everything at once, but you can take it step by step. Incremental changes every day will work in the long run.

Try to keep the momentum to get you closer to where you want to be. You can develop a plan to work on your habits and then pick one to focus on at the time. Commit to it!

BANNISTER EFFECT

One of my favourite stories, which I would like to finish off with and which I personally find very inspiring, is the story called The Bannister Effect. In moments of doubt or thinking that something is not possible, I always return to it and remind myself that what I might believe is not possible can actually be achieved. Before 1954, it was believed that running one mile under 4 minutes was physically impossible, that the human body could not possibly do it. In 1954, Roger Bannister, an English middle-distance athlete, ran it in 3.59 minutes, breaking what was believed to be an impossible record. But what happened next is remarkable – once it was known that the mile could be run in under 4 minutes, many other athletes accomplished it, and with even better results.

What this shows us is that it was not a sudden leap in the evolution of the human body that broke the physical barriers. It was a shift in thinking. Bannister truly believed that it was possible to run faster and break the record. He visualised himself achieving it over and over, and his mind accepted it as reality. The story also shows us that once we see that something can be done, something that was once believed to be outside of our realm of possibilities, we can also achieve it.

In our daily work or life, our mindset has the ability to limit us or set us up to achieve the impossible, not only for us but those around us, our team, our peers, and our family. We are in control of whether we will conform to what is socially accepted or try to believe beyond it. If Bannister believed that the record was 4 minutes, and nothing could be done about it, that it was a physical limitation, then he would never have been able to break it. He would never even have tried to do it.

Just like this story, what often keeps us from achieving what we truly want is the barriers that only exist in our mind.

To connect with Anna Griffin please visit
www.ReimagineThePossible.com

How To Do I.O.A.L.

A Simple Financial Blueprint

BERNARD H. DALZIEL

The tried and true principles of saving and spending less seem to be the only financial literacy that most of us are exposed to. For so many of us, that means we are armed with little knowledge about one of the most important aspects of our lives, which is how to manage the money that we all need to function and enjoy the experiences that give meaning and depth to our lives.

Throughout this chapter, I am going to share the I.O.A.L. system, one that focuses on four key areas that are critical to building your wealth and helping you grow your net worth. Along the way, I am going to help you gain a better understanding of how to meet your financial goals and positively impact your future. Let's get started!

THE BEGINNING OF MY FINANCIAL EDUCATION

I love to help others help themselves by providing solutions that can help them double their income and triple their time off. When I started out, it wasn't easy for me. I had a hard time growing up. I was definitely considered a problem child. In fact, I probably spent more time in the hallway than I did in the classroom!

Yet, that was not time that I wasted. Instead, I used it to dream and stretch my imagination, growing and developing my EQ versus my IQ. Since I was out there already, I got to know everyone. To me, a stranger was just a friend that I hadn't met yet.

I was ready to quit school at age 12. Yet, there were moments and individuals that helped me during this academic struggle. I had a counselor who taught me a secret that helped me to learn the 9 multiplication tables in seventh grade. At that point, I was skipping school on a regular basis. I was hauled back to school by a truant officer and assigned to a counselor named Tom. He became my friend, and told me that if I was determined to leave school, there were certain basic things that I needed to know, such as reading, writing, and arithmetic.

That was when he found out that I didn't even know my 9 multiplication tables. He helped me fill out a job application with a short quiz on it. One part of the quiz was the 9 multiplication tables. I had to write the multiplication table from 1 to 9, put four triangles in a square, and then mail it in. As I did the multiplication table, I counted down (see the diagram). Then I put an X in the box. Now I decided to mail it myself, but being dyslexic, I wrote my name and address on the front, and the address I wanted to send it to on the back. I forgot to put a stamp on it, but I did remember to put it in the mailbox. A week later, I received the call to come in for an interview for the position of an office boy. More about that later.

Notice all the things I did wrong, yet how it all came together. By putting the address in the wrong spot, but forgetting the stamp, the letter was essentially returned to the place that I wanted it to go all along.

I also read the book Psycho-Cybernetics by Maxwell Maltz. He was a plastic surgeon who found that individuals were no happier after plastic surgery, simply because they had changed their outside, but not their inside, which included how they thought about themselves.

I made the decision to change how I viewed myself. No longer was I going to see myself as an academic failure, but as someone with unique gifts and talents that I could share with others. I decided to dedicate my life to helping others to help themselves by providing easy to understand information. One area in particular that I knew I could help was by creating a simple formula that gives people a way to create a written financial plan or blueprint. It was meant to help them change the way they think about their finances and give them an easy step-by-step process for financial freedom and independence.

If the elevator for success no longer works for you, then I want you to have the ability to take the stairs, one step at a time. Most people don't plan to fail, they just fail to plan.

Granted, I still had obstacles and challenges to face. I was dyslexic, which made school a trial, as I mentioned earlier. Then I started down a self-destructive path, one that led to alcohol, smoking, and drugs. It was a way of life that could have cost me mine. Still determined to follow this path of self-destruction, I lost my father at the age of 15. Now, I had to stop doing drugs because I had to step up and help my mother. It was time for me to grow up. My mother, Irene Richardson, is an impressive individual, one who raised her children with a sense of purpose and a desire to learn. Even to this day, she is active, and her routine could wear me out! She taught me that common sense is not that common these days. At the ripe age of 89 years old, she takes no pills, just nutritional supplements, and leads a water aerobics class 6 days a week. Her one day off is for God, and she knows that God answers all who take a knee.

As I got closer to 16, I realized that I needed to be a man. I stopped using drugs and got my driver's license. I also joined the swim team. I truly started to take control of my life and shape it to fit my vision, instead of allowing others' opinions of my capabilities define me. By 19, I had taken the exam for industrial first aid, and I became a first aid attendant and night watchman.

Then I took on an apprenticeship and became a distribution engineer in Vancouver. At that time, I was making $50,000 a year. It was a chance to party, and I did that until I was 37. That was when I met my mentor Raymond Aaron, through his Dr. Al Lowry course on investing in real estate. I also took a Thurston Wright course. My world was on a high. I cleaned myself up, mind, body, and soul. I took a year off to work on my personal relationship with my daughter. At the time, I was earning $5,000 a month.

That was when life threw up a huge obstacle. My marriage was ending. The divorce was difficult, draining me mentally, physically, emotionally, and especially financially. Suddenly a judge was telling me that half my monthly income ($2,500) needed to go to my soon-to-be ex-wife. I was in debt and going through the divorce from hell when I reconnected with Raymond Aaron.

I signed up for his monthly mentoring program using my credit card. I was adding more debt, but Raymond told me to give him two years and I would be able to change my life. I completed the mentoring program and I still have the certificate hanging on my wall. I completed my divorce and refinanced my debts to a comfortable level.

The next few years saw my life taking an amazing turn for the better. I met and married the love of my life and was able to help her raise her son and godson. Both of these young men went on to receive Master's degrees in their chosen fields. My daughter became an RN and now I am about to be a grandfather. My life is rich and full of blessings, but I realized that now was the best time to reach out to others and share a way to make a financial blueprint simple. My goal is to make complicated things simple, and help us all to achieve a life of peace in the process.

One of the things I credit with helping me to achieve this level of success in my life is that I took advantage of having mentors. Too often, we assume that our experiences make us the best guide to create the future we want. I learned that this is not the case. Robert Kiyosaki, author of *Rich Dad, Poor Dad,* also served as a mentor for me. His cash flow game, and explanation of how and why we work, helped me to make changes in my mindset. I also found mentors in Brian Tracy; Fred Synder, a radio personality on *Of Your Money*; and Ralph Hahmann, author of *Pension Paradigm.*

Clearly, mentors helped me to define goals, create timelines, and stay accountable. I want you to find financial success, and that starts with tapping into the wisdom and experiences of others. If you would like to speak with me about mentoring, contact me at www.BenardHD.com.

WHAT IS A BLUEPRINT?

A blueprint is a planning tool or document created to guide you in the process of building or creating your financial success. It can include your priorities, projects, budgets, and future planning. It can be revised, but serves as a guide to help you understand where you are in your financial journey. You can also make adjustments or fine-tune it on a daily, weekly, monthly, quarterly, or yearly basis. This is because various factors in your life can change. My divorce was one such event, but I am sure that you can think of many other examples.

You could win the lottery and be a millionaire, or you could lose everything that you own to a natural disaster. Heaven forbid, you could get into a car accident and sustain severe injuries or, worse, lose a family member to death.

The point is that, whether you recognize it or not, we all have a financial blueprint, from the homeless man on the corner to the wealthiest CEO. It might be a conscious or unconscious thing, but it does exist. Others have it written down. What I am about to teach you can be written out by a 7th grader. Many of us don't have money problems per se but have accumulated a lot of debt and expenses.

I believe that if we learned this strategy in 7th grade, it could create a shift in how we handle our finances, allowing us to avoid the large amount of debt that most individuals carry today. What a difference we could create for the next generation by teaching them about saving and investment wealth accumulation, the difference between good and bad debt, and more. The point is that what you are doing now is based on what you were taught in the past. Yet, that is not going to help you to create the future that you want. The past doesn't equal the future.

HOW DO YOU CREATE A FINANCIAL BLUEPRINT?

Throughout this chapter, I am going to give you the tools to create your financial blueprint. I just want you to remember that you are trying to keep things simple, so don't be afraid of having to make adjustments along the way. As Raymond Aaron says, just keep failing forward. The important thing is to just do it!

You are starting on a journey, and you need to draw the map that will help you to reach your final destination. The phrase to do expresses motion or moving in a specific direction towards a person, place, or thing. The point is that you have to take action. Right now, you have to get out a pen and a piece of paper. I want you to get everything out of your head. Start with creating four quadrants, as seen in the diagram.

Next, I need you to collect information together, so you know how much debt you have and how much income you have, such as income statements, investment income, etc. When you do your first financial blueprint, I want you to go low on income and high on expenses. As you do the math, you will be able to see whether you are cash flowing positively or negatively.

Most broke people go high on income and low on expenses, then they wonder why they are part of the 80% of Americans struggling financially. Now that you are reading this chapter and committed to changing your financial future, you are on the way to creating meaningful change in your life.

The definition of do is to perform an act or duty, to execute a piece of work, to accomplish something, or to complete or finish it. I want you to see this financial blueprint as a means to complete the action of understanding your finances, so that you can make informed decisions now to create a different future.

It is up to you to do the work. I am merely here to provide guidance and inspiration as you follow the directions to complete your financial blueprint.

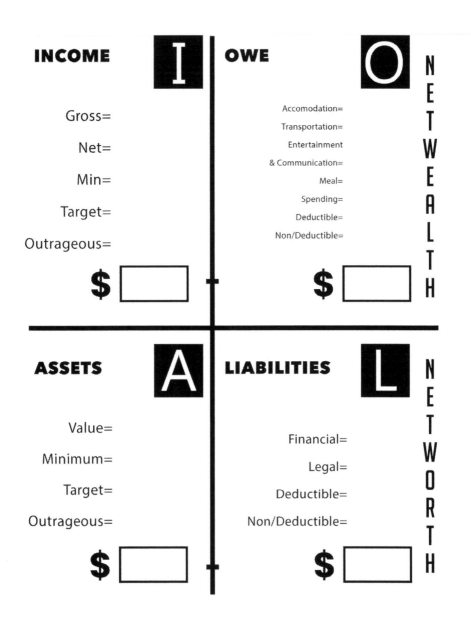

INCOME **I** **OWE** **O** N E T W E A L T H

Gross=

Net=

Min=

Target=

Outrageous=

$ [   ]

Accomodation=

Transportation=

Entertainment
& Communication=

Meal=

Spending=

Deductible=

Non/Deductible=

$ [   ]

ASSETS **A** **LIABILITIES** **L** N E T W O R T H

Value=

Minimum=

Target=

Outrageous=

$ [   ]

Financial=

Legal=

Deductible=

Non/Deductible=

$ [   ]

I OWE AL

My uncle Al gave me a simple way to do a financial blueprint formula. He explained that what goes in must go out. It is like breathing. The body must take in oxygen, in order to expel carbon dioxide. The concept is so automatic for us that, without even thinking, all of us take regular and consistent breaths throughout the day. Here is what is interesting, however. When we take the time to do conscious breathing, where we mindfully concentrate on how we breathe, suddenly the whole tone of our breathing becomes different.

You get more out of it, and your mindset shifts. You sharpen your focus and it proves to be beneficial to bringing peace to your mind and body. There are many different ways of creating this focus, a sharpness of the mind. I can think of several, including yoga, stretching, meditation, and more. The point is that you are creating an internal focus that can help you to achieve anything that you set your mind to.

The formula is I.O.A.L., Income (I), Out of Wealth (O), Assets (A), and Liabilities (L). Each of these areas is part of what you need in order to create wealth and grow your net worth. I am going to cover each of these areas and help you to understand this formula and how you can use it to benefit your financial plans.

INCOME (I)

What is income? Strictly speaking, it is the money that you bring in, either through your job or investments. Consider this the way that you breathe in, drawing in the financial capital you need to pay for your lifestyle, including your basic needs and your wants. Another way to look at it is the money that an individual receives from a company in exchange for goods and services. You are exchanging your hours and skills for dollars. The reality is that your income is often capped by the number of hours you work in a day, the number of miles you can drive, or the number of customers you can serve.

Investing, on the other hand, brings in money but the exchange is not the same. The rich use money to invest and make more money, often while they are involved in other activities. Instead of exchanging their time and skills, they are providing capital, and that means their income truly can't be capped.

Most of us think of our income in terms of what we make in an hour, multiply it by the number of hours worked, and then do the math to come up with our annual income. Yet, the reality is that you don't make that much. The amount that you did all the math to come up with is just a gross number and doesn't reflect what you actually get to spend.

What you need to focus on instead is your net income. This income is essentially what you bring home after you pay taxes, health insurance, and any other deductions. You might find that, in the end, your annual salary based on your hourly wages is significantly higher than what you actually bring home on your paycheck. Why is this important to understand?

Simply put, many individuals make spending decisions based on what they make in gross income and then wonder why they are struggling to pay the bills or meet their financial goals. They are focused on the wrong number, and its negative impacts their ability to grow their net wealth. Let's start by determining what your net monthly income is. I want you to write down every source of income that you receive on a monthly basis before taxes and deductions. Once you have that number, you can then subtract your taxes and deductions to come up with your net monthly income.

Now that you know what that amount is, it is time to look at where that income goes. Remember, many individuals plan their expenses based on their gross income, which means that they are going to find themselves in the hole every month. How often do you find yourself struggling from paycheck to paycheck, barely getting by, let alone putting yourself in a position to save and invest?

I want you to understand that just by acknowledging that there is a difference between your gross and net income, you are already ahead of so many individuals who are exchanging hours and skills for dollars. This is because you see the potential to rid yourself of the cap that comes with exchanging hours for dollars, and see the possibilities to increase your income with no limits.

When you choose to invest, it needs to be from the head and not the heart. Too often, people fall for a great story, but a poor business plan. Don't be one of them!

Pick your investments with an eye to the bottom line. What is the business plan, and what types of capital do they need to achieve it? Do their financial statements reflect a good use of capital, or do they struggle to make ends meet?

Consider using the Rule of 72. Einstein, who believed that one of the wonders of the world was compounding interest, came up with the rule. He explained that if you divide 1 into 72, then you get 72. So, if an investment pays 1% of interest, then it will take you 72 years to double your money. Now if that same investment paid you 72% interest, then it would only take you one year to double your money.

Recognize that there are wealth killers. These are taxes and inflation.

Working with professionals, you can find ways to legitimately reduce your tax bill. Inflation, however, is not something that you can easily control. Therefore, in the Rule of 72, it is important to use a 3% percentage for inflation. Essentially, now you divide 3 into 72 and you come up with 24. That means in 24 years, the price of everything will have doubled. Therefore, when you are determining whether an investment is a good idea, you have to think about whether your return will be greater than the inflation during the same period. If not, then it is not going to help increase your wealth but may actually decrease it.

It is a question of finding the right type of investments that can work for you, based on your investment knowledge and risk tolerance.

Additionally, certain investments can create a greater tax liability based on the percentage of income earned. Therefore, you need to work with a tax professional to determine the best ways to legally minimize your tax bill through deductions. You may also choose to sell an investment to keep your income percentage lower and thus reduce your tax liabilities.

Many individuals argue about the amount of taxes they pay, or see them as excessive. I am not saying that those things might not be true, but at this point, governments depend on the tax revenue paid by their citizens. Here is a point that I thought was interesting from the New Testament of the Bible. Jesus was approached by the Pharisees and asked whether he should pay a temple tax. Now the Jews had no love for Roman taxes, and Jesus knew that their motive was to try to trip him up.

Instead, Jesus had one of his disciples pull out a coin and he asked whose face was on the coin. When the Pharisees responded that it was Caesar, Jesus responded, "Render therefore unto Caesar the things which are Caesar's, and unto God the things that are God's." The point? That taxes and the expenses associated with them are what we render to the government for the services it provides. At the same time, we can render receipts or other documentation to reduce what we owe, just as I am doing to have a $20,000 tax bill adjusted.

Therefore, whether you like it or not, these taxes are going to reduce your gross monthly income for years to come. However, there are ways to reclaim some of that money through your tax-deductible expenses. Working with a tax professional, you can find the best way to do so, recognizing that there are legal ways to effectively reduce your tax bill.

Another point to remember is that not all income is created equally. What do I mean by that? You have interest income, wage income, and rental income, for example. Each of those can result in a different tax rate, with different deductions that are applicable, as well as different rules for what must be reported. Recognize that you need to understand where your money is coming from to achieve the wealth goals that you want in your life.

Our next section is going to focus on Out of Wealth Expenses (OWE), which is where the income meets the expenses.

OUT OF WEALTH EXPENSES (OWE)

Your income is your wealth, and it provides you a means to pay for the things you need and want. These expenses typically reduce your wealth over the course of the month. When you think of this aspect of the blueprint, think of it as breathing out, expelling your financial capital in a variety of ways.

Take a moment and write down all of your monthly expenses. The list is going to include your mortgage or rent, utilities, car payment, insurance, internet, cell phone, and whatever else drains your income throughout the month. There are also those incidentals that you don't think about, because they have become automatic. Your stop at the coffee shop in the morning for that amazing latte? Out of wealth expense. Your regular lunch out with your workmates? Out of wealth expense. These little expenses can add up significantly over the course of a month. You might want to consider making note of every dollar you spend over the course of the week. You may be surprised at how much money simply disappears without you being consciously aware of it.

Remember **ATEMS**:

A – Accommodations

T – Transportation

E – Entertainment

M – Meals

S – Spending

Each of these has an impact on your budget. For instance, accommodations often take the largest chunk of your budget, with transportation next, then entertainment, communications, data, meals, and other spending. This type of spending could even include buying chocolate from a child for a fundraiser at school. Other expenses can include everything from lottery tickets to coffee and medical bills.

Now, there are other expenses that many of us deal with. Student loans, credit card debt, and perhaps even medical expenses. All of it adds up and can significantly reduce your income. There are ways to reduce those expenses, including refinancing loans for a lower interest rate or reducing your credit card spending. You also need to find ways to pay down debt faster, because this will save you money in the long run. What do I mean by that?

Most debts involve paying some form of interest on the debt. It is how the lenders make money from the individuals that they lend to. Now some interest rates are smaller than others, and obviously, the better your credit score the lower the interest rate is likely to be. Why? Because the higher credit scores are seen as lower risk to the lender, hence they receive the benefits in terms of lower interest payments.

However, when your credit score is lower, your interest is typically higher, and it costs you more to borrow money. The best way to save money on interest is to pay more than the minimum and apply as much as possible to the principal of the loan. Doing so will reduce the amount of interest paid over time. I have seen several examples of individuals who end up paying thousands of dollars in interest on their credit cards, simply because they refuse to make more than the minimum payments. Do not fall into this trap.

The best way to save money on interest is to negotiate a better rate, and always pay more than the minimum. When you are offered great credit offers, be sure to read the fine print. You may find that if you cannot pay the balance in full by the end of the term, you may be facing higher interest fees.

Once you pay down debt, it is important to keep it down. There are two types of debt: the type that is for non-assets and the debt for assets. The reason this difference is key is because, when you create debt to buy assets, you are building your net worth. When you grow non-asset debt, you are actually reducing your net worth and lowering your wealth.

If you have written all those expenses down, including food, gas, and what you spend on clothes, then you know what your out of wealth expenses are. Is that out of wealth number lower or higher than your net income? If it is higher, then you are in good shape and can start looking for ways to increase that income even further through investing.

However, if your net income is below your out of wealth expenses, then you are going to have to make some adjustments before you can start actively building wealth. The first step was already done when you listed all your expenses. Look over that list and don't make anything safe. Everything has the potential to be cut. For instance, those coffee shop visits? Perhaps they need to be on the chopping block to give you back more of your net income.

Anything that is an expense should be on this list, but keep in mind that choosing your expenses can mean you save money, or you might find that you are spending more than you need to in terms of taxes.

Look at your credit card debt. Are you getting your credit cards paid down, only to spend on them again, perhaps even drawing them over the limit regularly? All of these areas are places that you can start to reduce your out of wealth expenses. The point of this exercise is not to deprive you of the things that make life enjoyable, but to look for ways to make your net income and your out of wealth expenses balance. Eventually, the goal is to make sure that your out of wealth expenses are significantly lower than your net income.

One of the ways to do so is by tracking your expenses. If an expense is tax deductible, keep the receipt and then use that deduction when you file your taxes. To do this effectively, keep all your receipts and then separate them with your accountant into two piles, tax deductible and non-deductible. You might be surprised at how many deductions you have that you may have never claimed before.

Understand that money for business-related expenses is likely to be tax deductible, but personal items are not. Pay cash for personal items and then borrow for business expenses, thus allowing for the interest paid on business loans to be a tax deduction.

Think D=Deductible and ND=Not Deductible. Clearly, you can see the benefits of being a part-time business owner, even while you are an employee. Still, to be sure that you are getting all the tax benefits from your deductions and to determine which ones you qualify for, please consult with a tax professional.

Why do you think the rich become rich and stay that way? Because they tailor their lifestyle to a portion of their net income and then stick to it. They look for means to bring down their tax bill and do the recordkeeping necessary to achieve that. Additionally, they look for ways to increase that income, which leads me to Assets (A).

ASSETS (A)

To put it bluntly, assets are what you could sell to pay your debts. It could be your home, your car, or other valuables, such as jewelry. All of these items are assets. Your ability to purchase new assets can be based on your net income, but purchasing assets allows you to grow your net worth.

Investments can be a way to create assets. For instance, you might have $100,000 to invest. Now you could buy a rental property free and clear for that amount, or you could take that same amount and use it for down payments on four other properties. The result is that you have significantly increased your net worth by the value of those assets, but you have also increased your monthly net income due to the rental income.

Assets can be collateral for loans, or a way to get a lower interest rate. Home Equity Lines of Credit (HELOC) are a great way to maximize the asset you have in your home. You can pay the interest only or pay the whole amount off at any time. It allows you flexibility to invest in additional assets over time.

Assets are a critical part of building your wealth. I like to think of them as an acronym for the types of investments out there.

- **A** – Accumulating
- **S** – Several
- **S** - Stocks
- **E** – Estates
- **T** – Trusts
- **S** – Securities

Note that the point of accumulating these things is to create wealth, by the income they produce and the value they have against the debt that you might carry to purchase them. Choosing your investments wisely can help you to increase your assets and positively impact your net worth. Every investment has a level of risk, but the point is to balance your level of risk with the return from that investment.

In real estate, for example, you are focusing on being cash flowing on a property. That means the property covers its own expenses and still provides a positive income to you. I want you to remember that investments will have losses from time to time, but the point is that you don't want to have to continue to put income into an investment, because if it is not increasing in value, you are losing money.

I want you to get off your ass and do something to achieve something.

Are you willing to step outside of your comfort zone and try different investments? It might include spending assets to build your own business. The value of the business can grow, thus giving you an asset for your hard work.

I pointed this out because your ability to grow your income and purchase assets will be limited by your net income. When you work a traditional wage job, it caps your net income by the hours you work and the size of your paycheck. I am here to tell you that business ownership can mean taking your net income and growing it with no cap.

Now you might not be comfortable running a business, or you might be unsure of how certain things work when it comes to running a business. However, that is why you need to be willing to work with professionals. They can supply the knowledge and experience you lack. Plus, you don't want to be doing every job involved in running a business. You do not have enough time or energy to achieve all of that. The term is delegating, and it is key to any successful business.

Remember, you are doing something to achieve the wealth you want. Start looking at business opportunities with a critical eye. What is the investment needed, and the potential rate of return? How long before the business would be cash flowing? You might find, for example, that a franchise offers you the ability to purchase a business with all the systems in place, which may reduce your initial investment. However, franchises can also limit your ability to make changes as you see fit.

Therefore, it is important to weigh your options before choosing a business to invest in or purchase outright. Plus, when you purchase a business, you take on liabilities as well. However, liabilities are littered throughout the different types of assets available.

Let's move on to Liabilities (L) and how they can impact your wealth.

LIABILITIES (L)

Part of the point of liabilities is understanding that they are the items that reduce your net worth and negatively impact your wealth. Granted, they might be necessary expenses, but the point is that they are reducing the amount of net income you have to build your wealth.

You can think of them as sunk costs, ones that you are not likely to recoup as part of your investments and wealth building strategy. It could be insurance, setting up a trust or will, and consulting with professionals to determine the best tax strategy for your circumstances. The point is that these expenses are not going to be recovered, but the amount of these expenses also needs to be monitored. You might find yourself spending more than you should on sunk costs, and that can negatively impact your wealth.

However, the real liability is when you lie about your abilities, and you limit what you are capable of. So, you take advice from broke friends and family members, instead of consulting with those individuals who are professionals and experienced in generating wealth. Here is where I want to encourage you to look for mentors or coaches, and follow them.

They have experience and knowledge that you might not, but they also can help you to capitalize on the knowledge and experience that you already have. These mentors have walked the path that you are starting down, and can be critical to helping you achieve your goals and objectives. These are the individuals that can give you encouragement, and can also hold you accountable for achieving what is possible in your life.

CREATING TARGETS TO ACHIEVE YOUR VISION

When it comes to creating more income, you want to have several different targets. I think of them as the minimum, the medium, and the maximum. The minimum is essentially what you are making as a net income right now, factoring in wage increases or perhaps additional investment income. Now you might set your minimum as slightly higher, so you have a goal to shoot for in terms of increasing your net income from month to month.

The medium is a larger goal, outside of your comfort zone, that makes you have to hustle a bit to achieve it. You might take on an extra project for additional income beyond your job, or you might find yourself investing more. The point of medium is to make you stretch yourself further than you have before. To achieve your goals in terms of growing your wealth, you need to be willing to step outside of your comfort zone. Medium goals are meant to be a driver for that. At the same time, when you achieve a medium goal, you feel the rush that comes from accomplishing something and it pumps you up. Suddenly, you can see that more is possible. That is where the maximum comes in.

Now I have heard this goal referred to as outrageous, but the point is that this goal means you are really going to have to stretch yourself and take a gigantic leap outside of your comfort zone. It might even mean completely changing your lifestyle to break the barriers keeping you from reaching that maximum goal. From month to month, you are going to be able to reach plenty of minimum goals and even a few of the mediums, but you might think that the maximum goals are just too far out of reach.

I am here to tell you that is not the case. In fact, every time you reach a medium goal, you put that maximum goal closer and make it easier to reach. Even if you don't achieve it right away, you don't feel like a failure, because you achieved one of your other goals. The point is to put achievement on a sliding scale, making it easier to keep yourself pumped up to achieve the financial goals and dreams that you have always envisioned.

Part of this process involves changing how you think about building wealth. You want to use your income to generate future income. Your wealth is going to be tied to the investment choices you make and how you use those investments to essentially fund the purchase of future investments. If your investments have investments of their own and you are living off of that income, you are generating a consistent income stream that will positively impact your net wealth for years to come.

As an investor, you also have the opportunity to have your money start making money for you by using a professional. It is important to remember that there are individuals out there who spend their days working hard at finding the right investments to fit a variety of circumstances or investing goals. They are going to listen to your vision and help you make smart investment choices to achieve it.

Interview people and find the ones who are successful. For instance, if you decide to use a financial planner, ask how much they made last year. If it was less than you, then that is not the person you want working with you, because he is broke! You want to work with successful people to achieve your own success.

One of the key points I want you to understand from this chapter is that, as an employee, everyone is benefiting financially but you! Self-employed individuals pay the same tax rate as employed individuals, but they get to take deductions not available to employees, plus they have a more flexible schedule. Business owners get even more deductions and tax incentives. Optimize your income by owning a business. If you are thinking that owning a business is time-consuming and you don't have the time, consider hiring a general manager to run the business for you. For more information about the benefits of business ownership to your financial success, visit my website, www.transformationalblueprints.com.

Then you receive the benefits of owning the business, while being able to collect the income and still pursue what you enjoy in life.

Your circumstances can also change throughout your life, meaning that your financial vision is altered as well. Working with professionals can help you to keep your investments in line with your vision, even as it changes throughout your lifetime.

CREATING YOUR FINANCIAL BLUEPRINT

Finally, I want to discuss how this all can impact the life that you live. Many of us have dreams and goals, but the financial realities are limiting us from achieving them. I want you to be able to live the life you have always dreamed of, and fulfill your purpose. To do so, you need financial resources. When you choose to work with a financial professional, you get access to someone who can help you to achieve the financial resources necessary to achieve your dreams.

You have the ability to create an amazing life, but you have to believe that you are worth it. Once you make that conscious decision, then the next step is to define what amazing is to you. Everyone's idea of an amazing life is different, depending on their own personal experiences, beliefs, and values.

I want you to take a minute and define an amazing life for yourself. I can give you one example of how I value myself, and what I believe is a critical part of my amazing life. I always travel first class. Now, it is more expensive than a seat in economy or business class, but I value myself and see it as a priority not to spend hours cramped as I fly. Granted, this might not be one of your priorities, but that is what makes this part so interesting. All of us are unique, and so each of our lives can be amazing based on those unique aspects.

Get excited about the possibilities. Define your amazing life and then act to create it. If you wait for someone else to give it to you, you will be waiting a long time. My mother is still incredibly active, living life to the fullest. It is an example that inspires me to get the most out of every day of my life.

I also want to stress the importance of finding support to create real change in your financial life. After all, it isn't going to be easy to change how you view money, how you interact with it, and how you invest it. In fact, you might be so focused on just paying this month's bills that you can't even imagine life more than 30 days from now. That is the mentality that you need to break. It takes conscious effort to create that mental change, to shift your mindset.

After all, it took years to create the habits and mindset that are now your automatic default. When you change the default, it takes time to make it permanent. To be successful at it, you must get started. Financial shifts require effort as well, but they are so worth it. Do not be quick to assume that you can't do it! Instead, focus on the blueprint and your action steps in each area. Perhaps you just focus on one area at first, then shift to another. Over time, you will see the change, and its impact on your life.

Throughout this chapter, I have shared key strategies and important information that can help you through the process of creating wealth and growing your net worth. It comes down to a simple formula, one that requires you to think in terms of algebraic equations. (And you said that you would never use that again!)

Income – Out of Wealth Expenses = Your Net Wealth

Assets – Liabilities = Your Net Worth

These two points are essentially your financial blueprint. No matter what you do financially, it fits into one of these four categories. The point is to make smart choices that positively impact these areas and thus increase your financial wellbeing. Go to BernardI.O.A.L..com to find more information on how this financial blueprint can help you to achieve success.

What are some ways that you can make real change in these areas? Let's look at all of them one at a time.

- **Income** – Look for ways to increase your income through investments or business ownership. These options allow you to use your money to make more money, instead of just putting more hours in at a job. Remember, you can only work so many hours a week, which naturally limits how much income potential is available at a traditional job.

- **Out of Wealth Expense** – Choose your priorities and then work to manage your out of wealth expenses. Always remember to live within your net income, not your gross income!

- **Assets** – Building a portfolio of assets is key to growing your net worth. Choose your assets, not only for their current value, but for how those assets can grow over time. Work with a professional financial manager to help you invest effectively to increase your net worth and build income streams that allow you to live the life you want.

- **Liabilities** – Not all liabilities are the same. Some are the result of doing business, including insurance and legal or tax guidance. Limit liabilities that drain your resources unnecessarily.

Each of these areas is part of making your finances what you need them to be in order to achieve an amazing life. I have focused on your mindset, on your choices, and on ways you can create real change. However, they all require you to get up and move. You need to act, to embrace your abilities, and focus on what you are capable of.

Too many of us sell ourselves short and end our lives wondering what we missed out on, because we did not embrace our abilities and talents. Don't make that mistake!

Granted, you might not be interested in an investment because it doesn't mix with your values or it is not going to get you where you want to go in the timeframe you have already defined. The point is to explore the options and find the ones that work for you.

I met a wealthy friend who told me about a great book, Rich Dad Poor Dad by Robert Kiyosaki. That book opened my eyes to so many concepts that before had appeared complicated. It was as I read his book and took inspiration from it that I had a better understanding of income and how to generate it, as well as the tax implications of that. Today, I help people determine the best investments based on their goals, helping them to understand how each income presents different tax rates and more.

Now is the time to act. Don't put it off until tomorrow or some future date that will never come. Instead, open your mind to the possibilities.

Years ago, a friend interviewed for a position as an office boy. It was going well, until she asked for his email address and he explained that he didn't have one. She politely said they couldn't use him, and that was the end of the interview. Instead of allowing a fear of rejection and the accompanying dejection take hold, he decided to get active.

He had $10, so he went to a wholesale fruit distributor and bought a bag full of produce. He then sold it door to door. That day, he doubled his money and a new venture was born. It took time, but he went from walking to riding a bicycle to owning a truck and then a fleet of trucks. His hard work created a viable business. Now, he could have let that interview bring him down but, instead, he used it as inspiration to move forward. I want to provide that same inspiration to you. I want to help you act to create your vision. Don't let the rejection get you and keep you from fulfilling your dreams and goals!

Let's get started working together as a TEAM (Together Everyone Achieves More). Please contact me at my website, www.transformationalblueprints. com, to create real change in your financial life, and discovering the resources to fund the amazing life that you deserve! In this chapter, I have shared how to map out your financial plan, creating a You Are Here point in your life. Now I need you to transform this moment, getting rid of what no longer serves you by transforming your thoughts and feelings, essentially exhaling your negative thoughts and emotions.

Part of that process involves taking action. What do you want to be known for at the end of your life? Name three things. Now is the time to create and build, so use those three things as a platform to get started. Let them help you to craft your mission statement and the theme song of your life. You are in control of your mind's eye, your dreams, and your creativity. These are the tools that will allow you to reach your destination and leave a legacy behind for generations.

Practice conscious bio-breathing. Take a moment to think about what you love, and then hold that breath and truly experience your thoughts. Recognize that in that very moment, there are thousands of cells are being born in your body! All those cells with be filled with the energy and information captured in your DNA. Now exhale on the negativity in your life, including jealousy, visualizing the cells dying and leaving your body within the time it takes to exhale. It is all mind over matter. If you don't mind, then it don't matter!

Life is a journey of experiences, but you are the one who takes those experiences and crafts them into a truly amazing life, one that will be a legacy for others to follow for generations!

Please go to www.transformationalblueprints.com to download the I.O.A.L. chart and to get more information and details about Bernard H. Dalziel.

Evolution of Consciousness for the Entrepreneur

Accelerate Your Consciousness, Master Your Life

AUDREE TARA SAHOTA

"Be the change that you wish to see in the world."

– Mahatma Gandhi

"With great power comes great responsibility."

– Voltaire, Uncle Ben Spiderman

We have been through the Industrial Evolution, the Scientific Evolution and the Technological Evolution. Now is the time for the Evolution of Consciousness. A term prevalent in the personal growth and transformational communities, the Evolution of Consciousness comes out of the ever growing New Age movement. It involves the process of self-awareness and the awakening of the human mind. In truth, it is about personally understanding and awakening to our own behaviors, belief systems and the answers to two critical questions: "Does this serve me?" and "Do I want to live this way?

What does this have to do with you, the entrepreneur? Self-awareness can be a powerful tool in the development of your success.

YOUR THOUGHTS AND BEHAVIORS CREATE YOUR REALITY

We are facing a critical time in our human history. I say critical because our economy, ecology and the human race are struggling for survival. The stress of maintaining your life and excelling to a better way of living has become unbalanced in the "me" culture that we have become. This struggle for survival has an effect on a personal scale: financial hardships, loss of jobs, market crashes, housing devaluations and a lack of well being. We are living fearful lives and have lost connections to both our inner selves and the outer world around us.

You can say that this cataclysmic way of thinking has gone on for centuries. Why do we now need to become aware of our behaviors and how we live? It is because all that we have accomplished, created and discovered can now be utilized for the self-preservation of the planet and the human race. We can take what we have learned and create a way of life that supports community, growth, prosperity and the regeneration of a damaged ecology. I see the Evolution of Consciousness as a coming together of all the past evolutionary processes, and the using of our higher awareness to shift and change the way we live in the world. We can then create a world where we are living to our fullest potential.

So, how does an entrepreneur fit into this world of instability and chaos? Every entrepreneur is a visionary. You think outside the box. Your thoughts and belief systems control who you are and what you become. You are looking for a way to succeed beyond what is expected of you. At the same time, however, everyone else in your life has his or her limited thoughts and belief systems. The outside support for your great adventure (owning your own business) is, therefore, weak, or sometimes non-existent. The evolution of your consciousness and the awareness of your mind's thoughts and belief systems will be your strongest supporter on the road to success.

Human beings are automatically hardwired for failure. It is ingrained in our being that we are less than perfect. Most people live their lives with minds full of negative thoughts. Those thoughts keep telling them they are not good enough, or that they do not have the power to create an amazing life. In fact, those thoughts often say "you do not deserve to have an amazing life". On average, people walk through life sick, poor and lacking enthusiasm or joy for life. They go to school, and then work at a job that meets less than their fullest potential.

You are the exception. For you, there is one big difference in life; you have a dream to do something different. You want to make a difference or do something better than anyone else does. How are you going to accomplish your dreams and live to your fullest potential with all the obstacles knocking at your door? The secret is to evolve your consciousness.

Consciousness by definition means to be aware or have self- awareness. To evolve your consciousness is to follow a process that leads to an unfolding of your self-awareness — that is, the awareness of how you live and behave according to your thoughts and belief systems. And, the evolved consciousness of an entrepreneur is a mindset that allows you to transform yourself continuously into the most successful you. You can then live your life purpose, be in a state of well being and accomplish your heart's desire.

Imagine what it will be like when you are acting and living in your highest potential. Your business, branding, marketing, the operations of your company and your relationships —with yourself, your partners and employees, your audience and clients — will all flow in an effortless way. Imagine your life flowing in abundance, with the ability to see your visions clearly and to manifest your dreams into reality. That is what the evolution of your consciousness will do for you. That is why your Evolution of Consciousness is the most important piece of the puzzle, your greatest tool for success.

THE PROCESS OF AN EVOLVED CONSCIOUSNESS

So how do you become this evolved conscious mastermind of business and personal success? How do you evolve into your fullest potential? There is a guided process to give you the tools you need to clear out the old patterning and create an awakening. The steps are:

1. Acquiring the knowledge or belief that everything is energy.

The first step involves understanding and adopting the belief that you are made up of energy. Actually, everything is energy — a vibrational frequency of wave-like patterns that make up our universe. Energy is an electromagnetic charge that is within and surrounds your body Material objects are slow moving vibrational frequencies (energy) that make up matter. Thoughts are fast moving vibrational frequencies that are invisible to the naked eye, but still move and create our reality. This concept is sometimes abstract, but there is a lot of information to research at your leisure. You may want to read about The Law of Attraction or about manifesting your visions into reality. You might also watch the movie "The Secret".

As an entrepreneur, your greatest tool will be your knowledge of energy and how to manage it to master your life, your relationships and your business. Energy affects how we are in relationship to ourselves and others. It impacts how we feel on a daily basis and how our vision of life's purpose or our business is projected and manifested into the world.

For example, there are some people who, for no reason, you just cannot seem to like. They are very negative, and you feel drained when you see them. Then, there are other people who you love to be around because they are happy, have a glow about them and are especially positive. You might say it's about how they act or behave, but it is really about the energy that they put out into the world. The same goes for your business. If you know about energy you can shift the energies in your life to attract the clients you want.

Importantly, your energy moves based on your thought process. That is why they say if you have negative thoughts you will get sick. This is true. Your thoughts create energy. In an instant, you can shift your negative thoughts to positive ones. And in turn you can change your negative energy into positive energy. In sum, *"Energy goes where consciousness flows"*.

Energy is an inherent tool at your disposal; a tool that, if you choose not to use, will be there anyway, reacting to your subconscious mind, an event, which you do not want to happen in your life.

2. Grounding your energy so that you become a stable force of energy.

Life is chaos. Constantly shifting, moving and changing. There is no way to predict or control what happens in your life. This is the cause of all stress, anxiety and grief. I see life, especially during times of transformation, as a tornado swirling around you. It becomes very difficult to deal with things or to make the proper decisions (or even function, for that matter) when life is coming at you like a storm. The drama of life picks you up and lands you in any place, usually on the top of your head. And, for an entrepreneur, this tornado takes on speed and velocity, tenfold. Flying by the seat of your pants is an understatement.

If you are not careful, the decision-making process can mean life or death for your business, your dreams, your life purpose and your financial stability. Grounding your energy will allow you to be calm and stable while the chaos of life is swirling about you. You can become the calm in the center of the storm. In this calm place, you are able to see the whole picture of what is in front of you, and you will no longer be held hostage by emotional reactions to any drama. There is a centered feeling within you, and that is when you will be most effective.

In my training as a healer, I have found that grounding meditation is the foundation for any energy/healing work. You cannot be effective at moving energy if you are not grounded. You cannot make important life altering or business altering decisions if you are not grounded.

To make stable calm decisions, your energy needs to be in your body. I know that sounds a bit strange but, as humans, we have the habit of moving our energies up and outside of our physical bodies. We are not even aware of what we are doing. The energy leaves the physical body because of the emotional pain and suffering that we experience from life; it is easier to cope when we do not feel the pain.

When the energetic body is not connected to the physical form, it causes the body to feel anxious. It can cause a sense of being out of control, unsafe. This experience may cause physical symptoms like heart palpitations and other unproductive side effects. Think about a balloon on a string that is not connected to anything else. The balloon floats away. That is your energy and your consciousness floating away and, with it, the ability to function effectively.

Actually, it is extremely important to ground your energy into the earth itself. Some people have done yoga or used other techniques, such as guided meditation, and imagined roots growing from their feet into the ground. These techniques are based on centuries old teachings that say to anchor your body energy into the earth about three to four feet. There is real science behind these practices. There are electromagnetic grids in the earth's surface, and we connect the energy body into the earth's electromagnetic grids. This gives us a sense of security, belonging and calm.

In 2004, while doing my grounding techniques for meditation and healing work, I discovered a relatively new technique. I was forced to go deeper into the earth to ground my energy. I felt the connection of my energy field anchoring into something very powerful. What I have since learned is that I was anchoring into a permanent electromagnetic field of the earth. Although there is no science as of yet to validate what I was doing, through time and experience I have found this to be a very powerful grounding technique. I have taught it to many of my clients, some with stage four cancers, some facing terminal illnesses (they are in various places of instability).

I also have used this technique with my clients going through life transitions and major upheavals, as well as with those needing to feel safe and calm before making important life decisions. My clients who have used this grounding technique instantaneously felt an improved state of being. There is no waiting; the improved state of being happens as soon as you do the technique.

And, with practice, this technique becomes so easy that it is requires just a quick thought to become grounded; your consciousness and your physical body are calm, centered and balanced in a way that makes you feel safe and unaffected by what is happening around you. You will then begin to live and function through non-emotional reactions to the chaos and drama of life. This will be a great tool in your daily functioning. And, it can determine your success rate in making important business and life decisions.

To learn about this technique and how to use it on your own, please visit **agilitrix.com.**

3. Using energy to clear your negative thoughts and belief systems.

The entrepreneur is a master visionary. The spark of his or her thoughts and the dreams that they build, lead to the creation of a product or business, to fill the needs of the many. Entrepreneurs go against society's grain and the protests of the subconscious mind. Then there is the ego; everyone is watching you, secretly wanting you to fail. Or your own self-sabotage tries to take you down — not to mention how nerve-wracking it can be to make all the correct decisions about branding and marketing yourself and your business.

As an entrepreneur, your mindset must be clear and clean of any negative thoughts. Since thoughts are energy, they can literally reach out and affect your relationship with the outside world. It is, therefore, imperative that you erase any negative thoughts from your mind. Being successful is based on how well you manage and clear your thoughts, your consciousness and your energy.

So, what are negative thoughts? They are the ones that speak to you in your mind and judge everything that you do. Sometimes they are things your parents have told you, or they are based on experiences you had in the past. Some thoughts are from you, telling yourself you are not worthy, good enough, smart enough, do not have any money; the list goes on.

Then there are thoughts of your own greatness, how amazing you are and how no one can beat you or your product. Those thoughts will get you in trouble too; in business a thought can keep you from paying attention to improving your products or services.

In sum, thoughts are your ego, and your ego is a manifestation of an untruth. It is how you perceive yourself and the world based on past experiences. The ego makes up stories for us to believe and cuts us off from having an experience based in the present moment. It is the ego that will destroy your hopes and dreams. This is not ego bashing; the ego has long served you and has been a great asset in so many ways. But it has been running the "show" for your whole life. Now, to reach your fullest potential and the best life or business you can create, your ego needs to take a step back. At **agilitrix.com,** I give you a tool to clear your negative mind set gracefully, quickly and easily.

The process of the Evolution of Consciousness is the empowerment of you taking responsibility for your life. You become the master of your reality and create the life or business that you desire. When you are aware of your negative thoughts and behavior patterns, and you make the decision to let them go, you move into a place of positive thoughts, and begin to manifest a very powerful reality for yourself. This reality is filled with a presence of your own truth, living in the moment and knowing that you have the ability and tools to have what you desire.

4. Manifesting your desires from the heart.

The concept of manifesting your desires (or creating your reality) is something that has been much talked about in the past few years. When the movie, "The Secret," came out, it introduced the idea that it is possible to have the life you desire by asking for it. In fact, "The Secret" became the most popular source of information on manifesting and The Law of Attraction. What the movie doesn't mention is that this information about manifesting your desire, is based in an old paradigm (knowledge) used in a time when the earth vibrated at a different energetic frequency. There is a science to it, which you can read about in detail in my book, *Body Of Light, the Evolution of Consciousness Through the New Chakra System.*

The crucial point coming out of that science is that something about The Law of Attraction has changed and, so, the technique for manifesting has changed. Now, energy is very fast moving, and that changes the way we relate to ourselves and each other. We are coming into the world of peace; we are shifting into an era of living in our hearts. Why is that important for manifestation?

The old way to manifest was to have a vision which would shift your thoughts and move the energy to create your desires. Easy, right? It works, but is problematic in that, often, along with the thought of what you wanted, came a thought of how it might be impossible or that you are unworthy, In that case, the negative thought canceled out the vision.

The solution in this new energy is not to have a vision. Instead, go deeper, out of your mind (where the vision is) and into your heart, where your desire is. Yes, the heart is where manifestation takes place in this new era! For a great tool to teach you how to manifest from the heart and experience manifestation in this higher vibrational energy, please go to (**agilitrix.com**).

To create and manifest what you desire into reality, it must be done from the heart. There can be no attachment to how it manifests. There is no business plan for manifestation. That is not The Law of Attraction. The Law of Attraction says like energies (thoughts move energy) attract to each other and what you desire will manifest. The most powerful energetic wave patterns are in the heart.

... the heart is far more than a simple pump ... (it is) a highly complex, self-organized information processing center with its own functional "brain" that communicates with and influences the cranial brain... These influences profoundly affect brain function and most of the body's major organs, and ultimately determine the quality of life." — **The Institute of HeartMath**

If you are going into business to create destruction or greed, the techniques I've been talking about are not for you; it won't work. Those negative emotions are low vibrational frequencies and thought forms and will no longer be tolerated in this new paradigm. However, If you are envisioning a business product or service to help make the world a better place because you know that you can improve on a system, or want to make a difference in the world and in your life, then this knowledge will work. These tools can only be used for the highest good of man.

Remember that the mind is not a perfected state of being where there are no negative thoughts. You must drop all of your vision into your heart. Breathe in your business plan — not the step-by-step process, but the end result of your goals and vision. Feel what it is like to have your successful business, all the support that you need and beyond what you can imagine. Expect that you will have the life of your dreams, feel what it's like to live in that place of complete happiness and then let it go. When negative thoughts come into your mind, use the tools I gave you to release them.

5. Stepping into the new paradigm of business and living your highest potential.

Once you have learned this process of understanding and harnessing your body energies for good, you will be able to create and manifest the business of your dreams — no, more than that — a business beyond your wildest dreams. This is especially true for entrepreneurs because coming from an evolved consciousness means that you will:

- Maintain calm and balance to make important decisions
- Clear your limiting negative thoughts and belief systems
- Living your fullest potential, vibrant and healthy — physically mentally emotional and spiritually
- Be able to manifest your desires quickly and easily

Nothing in your business, or your life, will ever be the same.

Audree Tara Sahota uses her knowledge and skill as a healer, reads the Akashic Records and incorporates her training in energy based life coaching into a formula she developed called Intuitive Strategies Coaching, please go to **www.agilitrix.com** for more information

Investment Success and Successful Beliefs

JASON G. CHAN

"**W**hy are you chuckling to yourself?" my brother asked as we passed by an upscale restaurant one night. "Did I miss something?"

"No, not really," I replied. "Remember those two Ferraris that were waiting for valet parking back by the restaurant that almost everybody who passed by, including us, were looking at and admiring? I just realized that if I wanted to, I could buy both of those Ferraris with cash, one for you and one for me."

Of course, I never did that. But that moment stuck in my head because it was the first time I realized that, financially, I had done okay for myself. I made my first million dollars investing in the stock market when I was just shy of 30 years old. My second million came shortly after that. That's when I stopped counting. I stopped counting because I finally found some comfort in knowing that my family was doing okay and that I was doing okay.

A few years before that, my father had suddenly passed away. It happened in 2008 in the middle of one of the greatest recessions in history. My family was entrenched in debt and my parents hardly had any retirement savings, let alone other investments. My two younger brothers and I were burdened knee-deep in student loan debt. I was living in my parents' living room because the basement where I had been living got flooded and became too moldy to stay in.

For most of my adolescent and early adult life, our family cash flow was tight, and we couldn't even afford a decent study desk. I haven't done too shabby for a boy whose desk was actually nothing more than a door flipped sideways and propped up by four poles on each corner; definitely not too shabby as an investor for someone whose degree was in fine arts and graphic design. I don't have a degree in business, finance or economics. I don't believe we need fancy degrees or education to do well in finance and investments or in life. For those who likes degrees, later in life I was told that I actually got a PhD earlier in life, since I was Poor, Hungry and Driven. At the end of the day, it's not your degrees or titles that make you, it's really about your vision and your beliefs.

YOUR BELIEFS ARE IMPORTANT

Sometimes people ask me what I did or what I invested in, hoping to get some insight as to how they too can achieve what I have. They're usually asking about specific things I did, specific things I invested in, or tools I used. What they don't understand is that these things are not the important part. Belief is where it all starts. To achieve investment success by having the proper successful beliefs, mental concepts, and proper mindset is the key.

After all, we all act and behave in certain ways because of our beliefs. Some beliefs serve us, some limit or deter us, and some set us astray. They shape what we do and how we do it. Before anything even starts, our beliefs tell us what we can do because they shape what we think is possible and what is not. Therefore, having the proper beliefs, or shaping what you already have, is really important in life, and also in investments. My purpose and goal is to help you adopt proper, empowering beliefs and realign, even discard, the negative ones as they relate to investments. It is only with a proper mindset and a successful beliefs system that you can get ahead in finances and achieve sustainable, consistent and long term investment success.

The first and, perhaps, the most important belief I want to share with you is it's possible for you to achieve financial and investment success. Not only can you achieve it, but you can achieve it on your own by empowering yourself to take control of your finances and investments. If a poor boy who started off living in a basement with a door as a study desk, who studied fine arts and graphic design, and who had large student loans and family debt could do it, so could you.

"It's Possible" is one of my favorite phrases from Les Brown. He goes on to describe that one of the keys to changing our belief system and enabling us to act on our dreams is knowing that something is possible. To know that a goal or that dream or that something we want or achieve has already been done or achieved by someone else, is to know that something is possible and achievable. More importantly, that "It's Possible" for you to achieve it too!

155

UNDERSTANDING FINANCE AND INVESTMENTS IS A LIFE SKILL

One of the first questions people come across when it comes to their finances and investments is, "Should I manage them myself or should I get someone else in the financial industry, such as an investment firm or bank, to manage them for me?"

Not only am I an individual investor who manages my own finances, I have also worked in the financial services industry, for one of the largest financial institutions in the country, as an investment sales representative for over 10 years. I am also a certified life coach who specializes in finance and investments. Through my various experiences, my short answer is that you should eventually invest in yourself and invest for yourself. Being able to take control and take charge of your finances and investments is a very liberating feeling that everyone should enjoy.

The investment service industry has a purpose and a place in everybody's life, but by no means should it be used or regarded as a long-term solution. It's like riding a bicycle with training wheels. Many people dream of financial freedom, but they are often dependent on an investment company to get them there. How could you be free and dependent at the same time?

Understanding finance and investments is a necessity in life. Just like eating and cooking, it's something we have to do for the rest of our lives. For this reason, I believe it's a life skill we should all acquire and develop. We have to deal with money, so we need to understand finance. Unless we spend every dime we earn or put everything under a mattress, we all have to invest. At the end of the day, nobody cares more about your financial future and well-being more than you.

HAVING SOMEONE ELSE MANAGE YOUR MONEY IS MORE COSTLY THAN YOU THINK

When it comes to eating, we won't eat out every meal, every day for the rest of our lives. We won't do that because we know it doesn't make sense and it gets expensive. So why would it make sense to pay someone else or a company to manage your investments every day for the rest of your life? Well, many people actually do that. One of the main reasons is because the investment industry has presented their fees in a way that seems deceivingly small and inexpensive. That's why many people don't mind "dining out" their whole lives.

Let's use the mutual fund industry as an example. The mutual fund industry is what most people are exposed to and familiar with when it comes to professional investment management. Aside from possible front-load and back-load fees and commissions, all mutual funds charge what they call a management expense ratio or MER. The MER alone for the average mutual fund ranges from approximately 2% - 2.5% a year. We'll take the low end of 2% to give them the benefit of the doubt. A 2% annual fee sounds small and nominal, doesn't it? The financial industry usually does not take the time or effort to explain what this fee actually means. Often customers are left with the impression that they get charged 2% MER from the gains that the company makes for them, if any.

In reality, that 2% MER is calculated and charged based on the entire amount of money they are managing for the customer, or what they call assets under management. What that means is, if you give them $100 to invest, they will charge you 2% on that $100, so essentially $2. Say you have $100,000 invested with them. At 2% MER, that works out to be $2,000 a year. For those who wish to have $1,000,000 ($1 Million dollars) a 2% MER would cost them $20,000 a year! To look at it from another perspective, a 2% MER fee in 5 years alone, works out to 10% (2% x 5). In 10 years, that works out to be 20% (2% x 10). In a mere 5 years and 10 years respectively, you would have paid out 10% and 20% of your hard-earned money in MER fees. Now consider that most people save and invest for retirement for about 35 years, how does the math work out for a long duration like that?

As I mentioned, the financial and investment industry is a business. Just like the restaurant industry and eating out, there is a time and place for services like that. However, it should not be used as a long-term solution, because it becomes very costly in the long run. I feel a true investment company and professional should be promoting financial freedom and independence, not financial dependence. Understanding finance and investments is truly a life skill that we should all acquire and develop. We can't afford not to.

In the examples above, I purposely kept the math simple and to the point and avoided financial jargon, such as compounding, time value, etc., because those are the kind of things that deter from the basic idea and confuse clients. The investment industry will critique our example and try to say that they will grow the client's money through the years. However, at the end of day, they cannot guarantee you any gains. So we won't factor that in. And to be fair, I won't assume they'll lose your money either. I kept it neutral in my example—no gains, no losses—similar to the "lost decade" that we experienced in the stock markets not too long ago.

INVESTING IS LIKE TREASURE HUNTING

When most people think of the world of investments and finance it seems overwhelmingly complex. A simple and interesting analogy I use to compare the world of investing and the investment industry is a big treasure hunt. If we were to look at it from this perspective, we would get a better understanding of how things work, many things would become apparent and begin to make sense.

So off to treasure hunting we go. Imagine we are in a world where treasure hunting is a big deal and almost everybody is out to find some treasure. Opinions on how to find treasure are a dime a dozen and everybody has their ideas and opinions.

Yet, despite the abundance of ideas and strategies floating around, many of these ideas tend to be passed around by people who have never found any significant treasure themselves. They hear and get these ideas and concepts from family members, a friend, a friend of a friend, and various media outlets. And where did many of these ideas originate from? A lot of these ideas actually came about through the "treasure hunting industry."

Yes, treasure hunting is such a big deal, there's actually a treasure hunting industry which is supposedly there to help you and guide you to find treasure. There are big corporate institutions with many employees who sell you treasure maps, treasure guides, strategies, tools and gadgets along with various products and services which they claim will help you find treasure. Many of them offer packaged plans to help treasure hunt for you through their professional and experienced treasure hunters.

The deal is that you put up all the capital to be used for the treasure hunt, but they do not guarantee you any success. The only guarantee is that they will charge you a management fee whether or not they find you treasure. And if they do end up finding treasure, they actually take a bigger cut of your money. So you put up all the money and take all the risk and they take a risk free payment from you in order to help you treasure hunt. And there are no guarantees of success. It's a pretty good business model for them, but not such a good business idea for you.

At some point you might begin to wonder that if these companies and their staff are so good at treasure hunting, how come they just don't focus on that and treasure hunt for themselves? Eventually, you'll realize that these companies actually make money from selling treasure hunting packages and products and by providing treasure hunting services. They don't make their money from actually finding treasure, per se.

Their frontline staff, sales representatives and professional treasure hunters, can give you all sorts of treasure hunting advice, ideas, and strategies, along with various treasure products and services the company has to offer. However, like most regular people, most of them have never found success in treasure hunting. The majority of their income actually comes from working their sales jobs and earning commission selling treasure hunting packages, products and services.

Sometimes you see some of these sales people enjoying the luxuries of life which can create the impression that they have actually found treasure from treasure hunting, but the reality is, they were actually just a successful sales person, not a successful treasure hunter.

Remember how we said that much of the common investment advice that floats around in public originated from these treasure hunting companies in the treasure hunting industry? A lot of the time this supposed treasure hunting advice is actually based on half-truths that are either outdated, have lost effectiveness, or have never been useful at all. They are mainly ideas and strategies used to promote and sell various treasure hunting packages, products and services.

There are actually really good and skillful treasure hunters out there. As you would expect, most of them spend their time treasure hunting for themselves. Some do open up treasure hunting companies to help others find treasure, but they usually require clients with lots of money and many of them have reached capacity and have stopped taking on new clients.

Keep this treasure hunting analogy in mind the next time you think about investments and the investment industry. It should give you an idea of how to make sense of it all and help you decide if you really wish to have someone else treasure hunt for you or not.

THE INVESTMENT LANDSCAPE HAS CHANGED

Since the new millennium, the stock market and investment landscape has been a lot different than it was in previous decades. This is not just a belief—it is a fact. It is important that we recognize and acknowledge this reality and incorporate it into our belief system for two main reasons.

First of all, in order to invest successfully and navigate through the stock market, we need to understand what kind of landscape and environment we are currently in. Imagine you are taking a road trip, how could you expect a to get from point A to point B if you were using an old and dated road map from many decades ago? I am sure it would be a frustrating trip with a few wrong turns here and there.

Secondly, understanding how the stock market and investment landscape used to be can help us understand where many investment ideas and strategies we still hear and read about came to be. More important is why they have lost relevance, effectiveness and significance.

Using the beginning of the new millennium, the year 2000, as a benchmark for the midpoint year of reference, let us take a look at the last 36 years of the S&P500, a popular and widely followed North American stock index. We will take a look and compare the 18 years prior to the new millennium and 18 years since the new millennium. So from 1982 to 2000, compared to 2000 to 2018.

In terms of returns, if you were to just buy and hold from the beginning of 1982 to the beginning of 2000, the 18 years prior to 2000, the total return of the S&P 500 was approximately 1,100%. From the beginning of 2000 to the beginning of 2018, the last 18 years, the total return of the S&P 500 was approximately 92%. A 1,110% return compared to a 92% return. That's a difference of almost 12 times.

In terms of declines and recovery, between 1982 and 2000, the two biggest drops were Black Monday of 1987, which saw an approximately 36% drop from top to bottom, which took 8 months to break even, and August of 1998 which saw an approximately 23% drop from top to bottom, which took less than 2 months to break even.

In terms of declines and recovery, between 2000 and 2018, the two biggest drops were an approximately 50% drop during the years from early 2000 to early 2003. If you happened to have bought at the peak, it would have taken you about 7.5 years to break even. Then an approximately 57% drop from mid 2007 to early 2009. If you happened to have bought at the peak, it would have taken you about 6 years to break even.

From 1982 to 2000, there was a 23% to 36% drop, with a recovery time of 2 to 8 months, compared to the years from 2000 to 2018, in which there was a 50% to 57% drop, with a recovery time of 6 to 7.5 years. From declines to recoveries, there was a dramatic difference in magnitude.

To summarize, it is important that we recognize and acknowledge that the investment landscape has changed a lot in the last 20 years because many investment strategies and ideologies we still hear today were developed during that comparatively stable and less volatile time. However, due to the changes we have seen in the last 20 years, many of these strategies and ideologies have lost their effectiveness, value, and relevance. The conclusion is, since our investment landscape has changed and evolved, we too need to evolve and adapt our investment strategies to the present. We cannot just keep on blindly using what has worked in the past.

WE INVEST IN OUR BELIEFS, NOT THE MARKETS

As we started off by mentioning, beliefs are very important when it comes to investing. They affect how we invest: if we take charge of our investments ourselves, have someone else invest for us or if we even invest at all. More importantly, I have to stress the importance of adopting the right and proper beliefs because ultimately when we are investing, we are investing in our beliefs. People often think they are investing in the markets, but actually what they are investing in is their beliefs about the markets. This is a critical concept to keep in mind. Personally, understanding and realizing that concept helped take my investments to the next level.

This reality might be a little difficult to wrap our heads around at first, but consider this, the markets behave the same for everyone. If we are just investing in the markets, we should all get similar if not identical results. But we don't. How come some people make more money than others in a rising market, for example? Or how come some are able to profit from a recession while others lose a fortune? The market's behaviour and performance does not vary from one person to another. It is the beliefs about the markets that vary from one person to another. Therefore, one of the main keys to being able to invest successfully is to have the proper beliefs in regards to investing and the markets.

GENUINE INVESTMENT ADVICE AND POOR INVESTMENT ADVICE

Many of our beliefs regarding investments have been acquired and shaped by various pieces of investment advice we've come across over time. And there's all sorts of investment concepts, strategies, and theories. Which ones serves us? Which ones do not? There was a time when it was tough getting information, let alone getting information in a timely manner. But today, with the evolution of technology via computers, smartphones and the internet, we live in a time of information overload. Investment ideas and strategies are a dime a dozen. Almost everyone seems to have an idea of what to do. We come across so many investment ideas and so much advice. Often, the more we learn the more confused we get, as many of these investment ideas seem to contradict each other. How do we organize and conceptualize them all in a context that makes sense? As an individual investor I, too, had to struggle with that problem.

After years of study, research and practical hands-on experience investing my own money, as well as working in the finance and investment sales industry, I was finally able to sort and put everything in context. This belief system is a mental construct meant to organize all the ideas, advice, theories, strategies, and concepts I've accumulated as they relate to investments. I'll just refer to all of that as "investment advice" for simplicity.

It's obvious there's some investment advice that works and some that does not. So, I separate them into two categories: "Genuine Investment Advice" and "Poor Investment Advice." Within those two categories, there are actually two sub-categories we could further separate the investment advice into.

Within Genuine Investment Advice, the first subcategory is investment advice that I believe is almost universal and works for almost everyone. For example, diversification, cutting losses short, letting winners grow, and waiting for favourable risk to return opportunities before investing.

The second subcategory, as well as all the other categories we'll touch upon, is where things get interesting. It's where it causes lots of confusion among people's belief systems and is a source of frustration for many. Within this second sub-category of Genuine Investment Advice is the investment advice that is accurate and works but may not work for everyone, because it depends on their personality and their investment style. For example, many investment ideas, theories, and strategies seem like complete opposites when you compare them with one another: value investing versus momentum investing, swing trading versus momentum investing, fundamental analysis versus technical analysis, short-term trading versus long-term investing, buy low and sell high versus buy high and sell higher, and top down versus bottom up investment styles. All these investment ideas and strategies work, but success depends on how they match the individual investor's personality and how they are used alongside their investment style. In a nutshell, those are examples of Genuine Investment Advice.

On the other end of the spectrum from Genuine Investment Advice we have Poor Investment Advice. It's basically advice that is not effective or does not work. Within this main category, it also has two sub-categories.

In the first sub-category is investment advice that used to work but is outdated because of the change in the investment landscape that we touched upon earlier. It used to work and perhaps even used to deliver great results but has since greatly lost value and effectiveness. Yet, these investment ideas still get passed around by many people because they have failed to recognize that the investment landscape has dramatically changed and evolved in recent years.

Some examples are: index investing, buying and holding indiscriminately, dollar cost averaging, and investing on a consistent and regular schedule regardless of overall market conditions. It's easy to see where such investment ideas, strategies and advice come from once we understand how the investment landscape used to be and what had happened in the past. Like we've seen in our example, the stock market, namely the S&P500, went up approximately 1,100% from 1982 to the year 2000. Yet, in our recent investment landscape from 2000 to the beginning of 2018, the total return of the S&P500 was a mere 92%—a return that's dramatically less than 1/12th in the same 18-year time span. That is less than 10% of the 1,100% return the we've seen from 1982 to the year 2000.

The second subcategory of Poor Investment Advice is the one which I despise the most. They are essentially "investment advice" that was never effective and never worked. For example, advice such as "If you don't sell your losing position, you aren't really losing money because unless you cash out, it's only a paper loss." That is as foolish as saying "If you go to the casino and convert your cash into casino chips, then you lose your chips, you're not actually losing money unless you convert those chips back into cash." Then there's "Adding to losses and losing positions is beneficial because when you average down, it gives you better value and a lower overall price point." With this strategy, you are not only not cutting your losses, you are adding to an already losing position. Technically, you could use this flawed logic to invest in a company as it goes all the way down to bankruptcy because it suggests the lower the price goes, the more you should invest. There is also "Focus on the long-term, and don't worry that your stocks are down because you're still getting paid dividends." Focusing solely on dividends presents a very distorted and partial picture, as you should be focusing on total return which consists of dividends plus any capital gains or losses. With that in mind, if your stock is down -40%, it would be foolish to say it's alright because you're receiving a 3% dividend yield.

People often ask, "If such investment advice doesn't work, then why do people say these things?" The answer is because these ideas mainly originate and get spread around by unscrupulous individuals in the financial and investment industry. In reality, such investment advice was merely conjured up to promote and sell investment products to customers and keep their customers invested so they could continue to charge them various fees and commissions.

Unfortunately, because much of this investment advice came from individuals within the financial and investment industry, it gave them a false sense of credibility and such bad advice got perpetually circulated. This is especially true because the advice is usually mixed in with some rationalization and half truths. When I say half truths, I am also referring to the dated investment advice that we mentioned earlier. I consider those half truths, because those strategies used to work, but have greatly lost significance since. Nevertheless, such bad advice is still often used as sales pitches by individuals in the industry to promote and sell various investment products.

Notice that all such advice falls under a similar underlying idea. It is to tell the customer that it is always a good time to invest and once they are invested, to never sell. For example, when the markets are high, they will say you should invest more because things are going well and you are making money. When the markets are low, they will say you should invest more because you are getting good value. Also, it is always a good time to invest, regardless of how the overall market condition is, because it is supposedly about your time in the markets, not timing the markets. Basically, the message is always geared at giving them your money, keeping it with them and never taking it away, so they can continuously charge you various fees. At the end of the day, if the client makes money, all the better, but even if they don't, the individual and company still gets to charge their fees.

In providing Genuine Investment Advice verses Poor Investment Advice, an individual's salary and bonus often comes in between the two. I'm reminded of a quote from Upton Sinclair: "It is difficult to get a man to understand something, when his salary depends on his not understanding it." However, to be fair, many of those who work in the financial and investment industry are not unscrupulous or ill-intentioned. Like many everyday people, they too, are caught up in the confusion. They come across poor investment advice that they actually believe to be true, which they use themselves and also end up passing on.

ADDITIONAL INVESTMENT TIPS FOR THE EVERYDAY INVESTOR

Make Use of Technical Analysis

As individual investors, we have limited time and resources. I believe the most efficient and effective way for an individual investor to conduct market research and to look for investment opportunities is through the use of technical analysis. Before you get intimidated, technical analysis is basically a fancy way of saying to look at price charts and graphs. You are literally looking at a picture, the big picture. It's efficient because, for example, if I wanted to, I could literally look through hundreds of companies and their price charts in a day. Comparatively, I cannot read through hundreds of annual reports or articles a day.

Keep an Investing Journal

Experiencing losses due to bad judgements or mistakes is part of every investor's journey. Unfortunately, when it comes to investing, making mistakes usually translates to losing money. At least when losses and mistakes occur, try to profit from them by keeping a journal of what happened and how, in an effort to learn from the experience and to not to let it happen again. As the saying goes, "Fool me once, shame on you. Fool me twice, shame on me."

Be Sure to Diversify

Diversification is a simple risk management technique we should all make use of to protect ourselves from the unknown and to improve our risk to return ratio. The simple reason being we can never foresee and predict everything in the markets. During my years of investing, I've seen an oil company whose oil rig was destroyed by a natural disaster; a factory that, due to some employee's negligence, was burned down to a crisp; the CEO of a company who got caught up in various alleged scandals leading to the collapse of the company and, one of my favorites, which is when Tesla's stock price took a sudden dive one day because Elon Musk decided to announce that the company was going bankrupt as an April Fool's Day joke in 2018. No matter how much in-depth research we conduct, nobody could have foreseen any of those events happening. So protect your investment portfolio by diversifying.

Look Beyond "Glam Stocks"

When individuals share their investment holdings with me, I often notice that they have many of the same stock holdings. The reason is they often have what I call "Glam Stocks." These are the glamorous stocks we often hear about in the news and media, the ones our friends and family talk about at dinner parties and gatherings. There is nothing wrong with having those holdings per se, but expand your scope, look further and dig deeper. You will realize that there are plenty of more diverse opportunities out there, many of which are either less volatile and less risky, have more growth potential, have a better performance record or sometimes all of the above. So keep looking and don't settle just for what you hear or see around you.

Know When to Get Out, Before You Get In

Before you get into an investment position, decide when you would exit if things do not go as intended. You are more clear minded before you start an investment. So decide when you would exit if things do not go your way ahead of time, as you will lose objectivity afterwards.

Gradually Ease In and Out of Investments

When investing, especially in stocks, a common practice is to use one entry and one exit into an investment position. Instead of using an all-in or all-out approach, a more strategic risk management approach would be to gradually ease yourself in and out of an investment depending on its subsequent performance. For example, instead of investing $5,000 all at once, consider investing initially only $2,500, then decide if you still want to invest the remaining $2,500 depending on the subsequent performance of the particular investment. Doing this would automatically cut your initial risk by 50%. The same idea applies to getting out of an investment.

Cut Losses and Keep Them Small

When investing, keeping control of our losses is a vital component of risk management. If there is one common piece of advice I've gathered from many great investors, it is that they all cut their losses and keep them small. Considering that most big losses usually started off as small losses, there is no point in letting a small loss grow into a big loss. If you are uncertain about an investment holding, instead of holding all of it or none of it, consider selling a portion of it. For example, if you sell half of it, you will reduce your risk by 50%. Another common culprit that leads investors to hold onto losses is focusing on break-even points and prices. In reality, nobody actually cares where or at what price you bought an investment and where you would break-even. It has no special meaning to anybody other than you and the tax department, so do not focus on that.

Avoid Adding to Losing Positions

When you have a losing investment position, often people believe that buying more will get you better value as you average down your overall price point. That is actually a poor strategy because having a losing position usually means that something you anticipated did not materialize and instead the opposite outcome occurred. There must have been something that was misjudged, overlooked, or unforeseen. Therefore, it does not make strategic sense to add more to an investment which you have already misunderstood and misjudged. Moreover, not only does that go against the concept of keeping your losses small, it is in fact the opposite, because you are adding more money to a losing position.

Remember that You Are Investing in Your Beliefs, Not the Markets

If there is one piece of advice that is more important than controlling your losses, it would definitely be that nobody cares more about your financial well-being than you. So understanding finance and investments is a life skill you should not only acquire but develop, and it all starts with your beliefs. At the core of it all, it is about working on developing your investment belief system.

This requires realigning and readjusting your beliefs and perhaps adopting new ones that serve you, while discarding those that do not. Remember that at the end of the day, we are all just investing in our beliefs.

FINAL THOUGHTS

Finance and investments are one of my greatest passions. I hope I was able to share some fresh perspectives and unique insights on subjects that I personally find to be rarely touched upon or discussed. The ideas and concepts are not exhaustive or complete, however, these are the big ideas, essential concepts and quintessential core beliefs that I've acquired through the years and which really helped propel my investment understanding and financial success.

Often there is nothing worse than to listen to someone advising you on how to reach your goals, when they have not actually reached it themselves. If there was a way for me to turn back time and have the opportunity to sit down with some successful investors who were willing to give me a few important pointers about finance and investing over a cup of coffee or a meal, I hope they would have shared with me the same pointers and beliefs I have shared with you in the last few pages. I know the insights would have definitely made my investment and financial experience a lot smoother and would have helped me reach my financial goals a lot sooner. These beliefs I'm talking about have helped me through many hurdles, make many investment breakthroughs and achieve financial success. I hope they will do the same for you. Remember, "It's Possible!"

For more investment insight, techniques and strategies, visit:

InvestingItWisely.com

Never Give Up!

My Journey to Purpose

VIVIAN STARK

NEVER GIVE UP: GROWTH AND SUCCESS COME IN INCREMENTS, NOT LEAPS

My desire is to encourage you with my life story. I have spent my life learning and improving myself, and I am thrilled to share what I have learned with you. Today I am living my definition of success. I have said NO TO THE PITY PARTY! Personal growth and development are a daily diet staple, and have fueled me in my business and entrepreneurial successes.

I wake up every day, knowing I am living my life with purpose, knowing I am the kind of person I always wanted to be. I have faced many challenges; my story has failures as well as successes. But I have learned that setbacks are only a part of the story; they are not the whole story. The story keeps going as long as you keep trying. You can choose to quit and make the story end in failure or dissatisfaction, or you can choose to keep trying and make your story what you want it to be.

Never give up. Success and growth do not come in leaps, they come in increments. The challenges will keep coming at you and sometimes it feels like two steps forward, one step back. But remember you did have those steps forward and you will again – if you never give up. You can choose to be overcome by dreck that life throws at you, or you can open your eyes to the love and opportunity that are always there too. You can have the life you want if you never, never, never give up on what is important – You.

IT IS YOUR LIFE - LIVE IT YOUR WAY

My life is my own for the making, but I did not always know this. I lived a very sheltered life as a child, fiercely protected by my overbearing Greek parents. I was not allowed to do the 'normal' girl things, like have sleepovers or join the Girl Guides to be a Brownie. When I was older I was not allowed to date for fear of gossip within my community. My parents lived in fear of the unknown. I lived in fear of being reprimanded if I disobeyed.

Despite my fear, insecurity, and extremely introverted personality, I pushed myself to exert my independence and fulfill certain goals that I set out for myself. From a very young age, I felt that I always needed to prove myself. To prove that I was pretty enough, smart enough, or even good enough. I worked tirelessly to achieve my dreams, never sharing them with anyone for fear of being ridiculed.

I began pursuing my goals as a young teen who wanted to fit in. I lived in an affluent area of Vancouver and always felt out of place. I did not have all the cool clothes that everyone else had, so I worked with my brother as a gardener cutting grass for one of my dad's clients. I saved my money and bought the clothes I wanted so that I would 'fit in' with the crowd. Despite this, I never felt that I fit in with other kids.

I was a rather "ugly duckling" as a younger girl, with a massive overbite and awkward shyness about me. After having braces, I felt my "ugly" stage was behind me and I decided to take a modeling class over several weeks one summer when I was in high school. My parents did not support me in this decision, so I chose to pay for it myself. The modeling class cost $800. I worked at Zellers for $3.00/hour. I persevered and saved enough money to pay for the class.

It turns out that the modeling class was just what I needed. I learned how to carry myself and exude confidence. After finishing the class, I took several modeling jobs and had many successes in my short modeling career. I made the cover of the then prestigious Back to School catalog for Eaton's Department Store, along with several other fun and exciting modeling adventures.

My modeling highlight and a fond memory was when I was hired for a ski catalog. (They wanted a curvy model. Who knew that sometimes it pays to not be super skinny!) We were taken up to the top of Blackcomb Mountain by helicopter before the official ski season opening. I remember having to jump out of the helicopter into three feet of snow because the helipad was snow-covered, and the helicopter could not land. I was paid $850 per day for three days. It was a dream come true. I felt validated.

When I was nineteen I began dating a handsome Greek guy I met at a wedding. Before I knew it, his parents and my parents got together and began planning our wedding. I literally cannot remember him actually asking me to marry him. How sad is that? Some time before our wedding I found out that he was into drugs and was still seeing his ex-girlfriend. I broke up with him and cancelled the wedding.

To escape well-meaning friends and relatives, I took an extended holiday to Greece where I could recover from the breakup. Armed with my modeling composite cards and my lovely, fashionable clothes, I hoped to land some modeling jobs while I was there. Instead, I met another handsome Greek guy who was smooth and charming. He swept me off my feet.

In classic old-school Greek fashion, my mom flew to Greece to check him out and determine whether he was a suitable partner for me. Like I said, I lived a sheltered life. She approved and, after a civil wedding in Canada, I moved to Greece to start my life with my new husband.

The first thing he did when we settled in to our home was give away all my beloved clothes. He proceeded to tell me what I could and could not do, where I could and could not go, and how I had to act. He, like my parents, was consumed with what other people thought of him and now me. I was terrified. What had I done?

I realized very quickly I had made a huge mistake and wanted to leave him and go back to Canada. To my surprise, I was already pregnant. Too embarrassed to tell anyone my sad state of affairs, I stayed in Greece. I had made an agreement with my husband that our children would be born in Canada. I did not want to risk my children having to go to the army if they were boys. After my first son was born, I returned to Greece.

When I became pregnant with my second son, I decided to leave Greece, not to return. I told my husband I was going back to Canada and he could come with me or not. He chose to move to Canada with me, but we broke up after a few years. Our marriage was just not meant to be, but I was blessed with two healthy, adorable and rambunctious boys that I loved so much.

Once divorced, my husband went back to Greece to avoid paying child support and to be near his momma, so she could pamper and take care of him. (It's a Greek thing. He was a huge momma's boy. Never again.) I was determined that my two boys would never be momma's boys!

THE SETBACK IS NOT THE END OF THE STORY
PUSH YOURSELF TO YOUR NEXT GREAT CHAPTER

For the next few years, I lived in low-income housing while raising my boys and working at Woodward's department store. Then, I left my job at Woodward's and began a career in banking. I started out on the front lines working as a teller. After six weeks I was promoted to the prestigious side counter position. Within a year I was promoted again to managing tens of millions of dollars of lawyers' trust funds in an exclusive, independent position.

I was always pushing myself to be better, to do more, be more, have more so I could give more. I wanted to improve myself and my income to support my family. I had an internal drive to never give up. I wanted to prove everyone wrong. I would make it. I could do this! During these years I learned to appreciate life's lessons and gifts and I continued to grow.

Ten years after my first marriage, I married a second time. I became pregnant soon after our wedding in Hawaii but spent most of my time during our marriage being neglected by my husband. As soon as my daughter was born, I no longer existed in his eyes. I later found out that my husband had a girlfriend before, during, and after our entire marriage. He worked with her; she was married, too, and the four of us occasionally hung out together as couples. Needless to say, the marriage did not last, but I would not change a thing as I have my beautiful daughter from that relationship.

I spent the next years relentlessly trying to find my passion. I worked in banking, direct sales, office supplies, a genealogical search company, and as a sales manager for a roofing distribution company. I also went to night school while working full-time and raising my kids, to get my diploma in International Trade. Additionally, I began a calling card company in Santiago, Chile that I launched at the Canada/Chile Trade Mission in 2003.

OPPORTUNITY KEEPS KNOCKING, SO OPEN THE DOOR!

I was very proud of the calling card company. It was a crazy dream, but I wanted to make it happen. Recognizing a huge opportunity, I wanted to offer an affordable service that we took for granted in Canada. The large telecommunications companies had a very different view on my entry to the marketplace and I was forced out of business when they pressured my distribution channel to drop me. Unfortunately, my venture was short-lived after significant effort and money had been invested. I planned to travel back to Chile to negotiate a deal with another distributor when I was rear-ended in a car accident and suffered severe whiplash, leaving me unable to travel. I had to move on from this company but by this time I knew it was not the end. I knew other opportunities would come my way.

By 2007, I was working for a computer company selling proprietary software and hardware for restaurants. My expertise in sales and customer service had grown significantly by then. I had come a long way from the introverted little Greek girl who thought she was not good enough. With perseverance, training, and a belief in myself I had become a great salesperson.

I loved working with customers and was enjoying my new career when I began having severe migraines regularly. I was also having issues with my sinuses. I thought I probably had a severe sinus infection, but my nose and upper gums were numb, which was troubling.

That August was one big headache, literally. I had eight migraines that month and each one put me down for two to five days. I went to the doctor and had several tests run, including a CT scan. After the CT scan doctors finally determined the cause of my sinus trouble and migraines.

I will never forget that day. The doctor's office called and scheduled me for a 7:00 PM appointment. The doctor came in and told me that I had a brain tumor and that she was very sorry, but she did not know whether it was benign or malignant. She had not consulted a neurologist before meeting with me. I drove home in a state of shock and called my mom to tell her the news.

I learned that I had a meningioma, a benign brain tumor. After an MRI, I learned it measured 3.3 x 3.4 x 4.4 cm, was in my right frontal lobe, and had probably been growing for twenty or thirty years. Only recently had it grown large enough to begin causing migraines, sinus pain, and facial numbness.

Within a month I would be having major brain surgery to remove the tumor. Oddly enough, I was not scared until the day of the surgery, when it really sunk in. I had been told that the tumor was in an excellent location for surgery and that I would not need chemo or radiation afterwards. The tumor was not going to kill me. But with any surgery there is always a risk.

I do not remember much that happened the first week or so post-surgery. When I really came around and began noticing things, the first thing that caught my attention was that I was having significant vision problems. The brain surgeon had touched a nerve in my right eye, causing fourth nerve palsy. I always had this weird talent to do crazy thing with my eyes and move them independently, but this was something I could not control. I had severe double vision. I could only see straight when I looked through a very narrow view if I tilted my chin down. And I could not look to my left at all. When I tried, I lost all focus and control of my eyes.

This condition is similar to a child having a wandering eye. Actually, I had to be seen at Vancouver Children's Hospital to have my condition monitored. This was a very challenging time for me. It was one of the worst times of my life. I had so much stress and anxiety wondering if my vision would be like this forever. My head was permanently disfigured, leaving my self-esteem at an all-time low. My jaw was so stiff from surgery that I could barely open my mouth to eat. I was house-bound, and unable to walk up or down stairs without assistance. I could not read or watch TV to occupy myself because I was constantly dizzy. Every negative thought you could possibly imagine ran through my mind thousands of times each day. I wish I had known then what I know now about keeping a positive mindset, the healing powers of affirmations, an attitude of gratitude, and the law of attraction.

I cannot stress enough how important it is to reach out to family and friends to help you during a medical crisis (or any crisis, for that matter). Having people who love you to support you is so important. Being the independent person that I am, I did not ask for much help. Silly me. Stupid me, actually. I did not want to worry my kids any more than they already were. My mother was such an angel. She lived nearby and prepared meals for us, but for the most part, I was alone in my thoughts in a very dark place.

About five weeks into my recovery, I met someone online. Bored out of my mind, I had gone on a dating site, half-blind, looking for strangers to converse with me. Talk about being desperate! For our first meeting, I rode the bus to downtown Vancouver where we met for a drink. He must have thought I was rather forward on a first date when I grabbed his arm to walk up a few stairs. Little did he know that I grabbed his arm so that I would not fall flat on my face.

We hit it off and developed a relationship. He picked me up every day for several weeks and took me out on his random errands just to get me out of the house. Sometimes we would just hang out. At first, I only told him that I'd had a recent eye surgery. Eventually I told him the extent of the surgery. He was also having some challenges in his life, so it was wonderful to be able to help each other. I cannot tell you what a godsend he was for me. He came into my life exactly when I needed him, and I am forever grateful for what he did for me.

Worried about losing my job, I returned to work twelve weeks post-surgery. I was worried about paying my bills and the mortgage on the house I had recently purchased. I needed the money, or so I thought. In hindsight, that was the worst decision I could have made. I suffered with migraines and vision issues for several weeks before the universe decided I'd had enough. All of the senior managers, including me, were laid off from our jobs. It was the biggest blessing.

I did not work for two years. It was a very trying time. The line of credit was on a steady increase as the months went by, but I needed to heal. My vision took over a year to somewhat normalize, and the severe numbness in my face post surgery lasted for several years.

During this period, I had a lot of time to think. My surgery was a life-changing experience. I could have died. I decided to take on a totally different view on life from this time forward. From this point on, any time an opportunity presented itself I was going to take it.

DEFINE YOUR WORK AND WHAT YOU NEED

Knowing that after all my health problems I would need a job that allowed me to make my health a priority, I decided to choose a job that would work for me rather than choosing to work for the job. I started slowly by taking a 100% sales commission, part-time position that allowed me to work as much or as little as I wanted.

I told my bosses about my medical condition, and that I was not sure how I would respond to being back to work. My boss told me that as long as I was meeting or exceeding my quotas that he would not micromanage me. I would be allowed to do my own thing, which was perfect for me. For some this would be a scary venture to undertake, but I was up for the challenge.

I pushed myself by working long hours, often answering customer emails at 6:00 AM before I went to work and again well into the evening. I needed to build up my customer base and wanted to ensure they were well taken care of. Within less than six months I was working full-time and making a full-time income. I was back!

After working for this company for about four years, a couple of millennials were hired into the mix, and that changed everything for me. I was working independently with little interaction with my bosses for the most part and the millennials were cc'ing him on every email they sent. This is when my interest in generational differences in the workplace was first piqued.

Although I enjoyed the work and my co-workers, my bosses were a different story. My work environment left much to be desired. Receiving year-end bonuses based on sales is a standard practice in the world of sales. When I did not receive a bonus at the end of 2013 because my boss said I was "already making too much money," I decided to look at other business opportunities. Forever the entrepreneur!

I continued working my sales job while seeking other opportunities. I joined an Australian direct sales company and quickly rose to the top of their company, becoming one of their top 20 earners out of 20,000 consultants. I had 1,700 consultants on my team and was the only director in North America. I earned free trips to Australia, Dubai, Aruba, Florence, Manchester, Dallas, and Los Angeles. I finally left my sales job in 2016 to pursue my new business venture full-time.

DREAM BIG AND HELP OTHERS DREAM TOO

I LOVED working with my team. Coaching and mentoring were my passion. In October 2016, I attended a One Day to Greatness seminar with Jack Canfield in Kamloops, BC. After a brief conversation with Jack, I decided to take his Train the Trainer course to become a certified Success Principles Trainer. The intention was to share this new knowledge with my team. I had found purpose and passion in supporting others to build successful teams. I felt fulfilled when I saw their self-esteem and confidence grow. They were conquering their fears and winning!

Unfortunately, I had to resign from the direct sales company in February 2017 when they started having issues with production and delivery. Later that year the company declared bankruptcy. I went through a lot of stress, anxiety, and loss of sleep. Panic attacks became the daily norm for me. I had known the CEO for over eighteen years and was completely in the dark about the state of the company. My team was upset and blaming me. I received a constant stream of Facebook messages and harassing emails. The downfall of the company was out of my control, so I had to bow out. But this was not my first time at the rodeo. I knew that my story did not stop here if I chose to keep trying.

I met someone in late 2016 who introduced me to an opportunity to speak and train businesses on generational differences in the workplace. I was fascinated by this as I saw the struggles my own millennial children were having at work. I look back now at the communication challenges that existed in my previous jobs and wish I knew then how the different generations think and process information. I wanted to more closely understand their environment and what I could do to help. It made perfect sense that bridging the generation gap would improve productivity, communication, collaboration, and make for a happier, more cohesive work environment.

I now know that the behaviors, attitudes, beliefs, experiences, and influences during an individual's formative years really shape who they are and how they behave in all areas of their lives. I was excited about my new-found knowledge, and planned to launch my speaking business by mid-2017.

I hired an image consultant to come to my home and do a complete wardrobe change to prepare me for my speaking career. Having someone go through my wardrobe and tell me to get rid of most of it was a very difficult experience. There were a few tears. I must have attachment issues! I eventually embraced the change and spent thousands of dollars on a new wardrobe to complete my new look.

Then, as luck would have it, I broke a veneer on my front tooth. No big deal, I thought. I had been through this before and would just have it replaced.

This was the beginning of my dental nightmare. From May 31, 2017 through December 21, 2017, I had twenty-six dental appointments to fix my front tooth. I began lisping and developed what doctors believe is a stress-related condition. I lost the saliva in my mouth, had burning in my throat from acid reflux brought on by stress, my voice was constantly hoarse, and I spent several months waking up with panic attacks. I never knew from one to day to the next if I would have a voice or not, so I had to put everything on hold.

I saw every doctor and specialist I believed might be able to help me. I was taking six pills a day to help with my various symptoms. I hated this! I needed to feel better; I needed to heal my body naturally. I would not stop until I got the answers I needed. I moved away from traditional medicine, stopped taking all my medications, and began incorporating EFT (Emotional Freedom Technique), also known as Tapping, Reiki, and Bioenergy work, to heal my body.

Eventually, my body and voice were getting to the point where I could speak relatively well, I decided to move forward with the training business. I hired a business coach to get me on the right track, mentally and physically. He helped me tremendously during a very difficult time. I also attended Raymond Aaron's Speaker and Communication Workshop, which totally changed my training and speaking style. It gave me the confidence I was lacking and sent me on a whole new trajectory for my business. I began my own company, Gen-Connect Training in early 2018. It has been an amazing ride. I am much more at peace and ready for the next stage in my life.

LIVING IN THE POSITIVE HAS MADE MY LIFE

Although I have been blessed with many struggles, I have also enjoyed many successes. I have experienced relationships that did not work out, work and business challenges, worries when raising three children as a single parent, medical challenges, and many dreams and goals that seemed impossible. The one thing I always knew for sure was that if I gave up and wallowed in self-pity, I would be letting myself and my children down. That was not an option. Success was the only acceptable outcome.

I wanted to show my children what a strong, self-sufficient and resourceful mother I could be, and that they could always rely on me. I wanted to set an example and prove to myself and my children that I could provide for us no matter what. I am very proud of the amazing people my children have become; they are strong, independent, kind, respectful, and loving. This is the true meaning of success for me. Out of all the things I have accomplished thus far, they are my crowning glory.

FIVE STRATEGIES FOR A SUCCESSFUL LIFE

1) **Always have a positive mindset.** This is a crucial component. Before you get into the power of a positive mindset and the law of attraction, spend some time listening to what you are currently telling yourself. Check in with yourself. What is going on with you? We constantly speak to ourselves with an inner voice which is sometimes quietly whispering and sometimes yelling. Once you have spent a few days noticing how you speak to yourself, you may not like it very much; after all, you are your own worst critic. Be accountable for how you speak to yourself. Never fear, you have the power to change that inner voice!

Do you believe you are the product of everything that has happened to you in your life? Your inner voice may try to convince you that you are a victim of your circumstances and your past. Reflect and acknowledge the things that have happened to you and where you are now. Then prepare to move past them.

2) Shift your mindset using the law of attraction. You can influence things around you so that things happen FOR you rather than TO you. The universal principle of the law of attraction is that 'like attracts like.' The law of attraction manifests through your thoughts by drawing to you not only thoughts and ideas that are alike, but also people who think like you, along with corresponding situations and possibilities. It is the magnetic power of the universe which draws similar energies to each other.

The law of attraction is already working in your life, intentional or not. If you have a negative mindset, many unpleasant or unwanted things are probably happening in your life, and you may see negative things happening all around you. Think back to how you speak to yourself. Be mindful of your thoughts and that inner voice. Begin to think positively.

Along with thinking positively, begin to intentionally think and feel the things that you would like to have in your life. The most common things people desire are love, a career, good relationships, health, and wealth. Visualize a mental image of what you want to achieve. Repeat positive, affirming statements to create and bring into your life what you visualize or repeat in your mind. In other words, use the power of your thoughts and words.

Imagine that what you desire is already a part of your life. Acknowledge it with each of your five senses, to the extent that you can. Spend time imagining your life once you have acquired what it is that you want. Write out your affirmations and read them aloud at least once daily. You will begin to draw them to you when you act as though you already have what it is that you want. Persistence is key!

3) Take calculated risks. Do you encourage yourself to stay where you are and play it safe? Safe can be dangerous. I encourage you to take calculated risks. If you do not try new things you will never know how far you can go. When opportunities present themselves, jump on them. It may be your one and only chance. Push yourself and do not take no for an answer. Keep digging until you find the answer you want.

Quitting is always an option. Well, it is an option for those who are content living a mediocre life. Quitting is an option unless you want to live an amazing life with a purpose. If you want to live the life of your dreams, you must not give up. Do not give up and never stop learning. If you continue to learn, you will continue to grow both personally and professionally.

4) Appreciate all of life's lessons and gifts with an attitude of gratitude. Learn and grow from your failures. Let life's challenges teach you to persevere even when all you want to do is give up. Remind yourself that the only outcome you will accept is success.

5) NEVER Give Up. We all face adversities and challenges in life. It takes character, drive, and a positive mindset to persevere, overcome, and excel in life. The only person who can stop you from achieving your goals is you. If I can do it, so can you. Go for it!

Do you, your team, or organization want to be inspired to change your future and find your purpose?

Do you want to learn how mastering the Five Strategies for a Successful Life can empower you in both your personal and professional career?

Do you want to say "NO TO THE PITY PARTY" and achieve the life you truly desire?

Vivian Stark is an inspirational speaker and corporate trainer living in Vancouver, B.C. Canada, whose captivating story will inspire you to live the life you want if you never, never, never give up on what's important – You.

As a generational and workplace effectiveness expert, Vivian's career centers around helping others work in a more collaborative and cohesive work environment. Her focus on engagement and accountability both in and outside of the workplace mirrors her personal belief of how you must take 100% responsibility in all areas of your life. Learn how giving up blaming, complaining and excuse making can lead you to live a life filled with peace, happiness and personal fulfillment.

To learn how you can incorporate her knowledge and expertise into your life and business with ease and confidence, reach out to Vivian at www.gen-connect.ca. Vivian is available for private or corporate speaking engagements.

Power, Purpose and Passion

TONY DAVIS

Many people struggle in the maze that's the rat race of life. They feel like they're missing some vital clue that would release them from the endless corners and dead-end stretches. They might not enjoy their work, or they may be putting in too many hours of their time or there may not be enough dollars left over at the end of each month. Life often seems complicated and difficult to balance. Yet, when I ask people what they wanted to be when they grew up, the answer is typically a job (a doctor, fireman, architect, etc.). Why is this? Why should your job define who you are as a person? Why is the answer not to be a good person? Or, a great husband? Or, to be in love? We all have gifts and talents that we can use to be impactful in both work and life. So why do only a minority of people ever reach their full potential? The answer is quite simple. They fail to utilize the gifts and talents I just mentioned. In fact, it's often the first place people go wrong when creating their self-definition. It's a misalignment that can easily complicate and disorder life. On the other hand, when you're able to form a connection between what you love, your gifts, talents and purpose, not only will you be put on a path towards a more prosperous career, but it will also be a significant one—a life you love and of which you're proud. This chapter will show you how to make this connection by aligning your power, purpose and passion for leading a more fulfilling and successful life.

THE CORE

To avoid falling into the trap of defining yourself by the wrong things (and the problems associated with doing so), you need to find what's at your core. However, it's challenging to make it through this maze without knowing your end goal. Money and work are essential parts of life's puzzle, but they aren't the only things that matter. Your dreams and your passions are also pieces. In life, you'll often set a goal and see this as an ideal. You'll choose a college major, for example. You'll then work to finish it, get a job in that field and, after a while, what you had felt was ideal might start feeling like an ordeal. In this type of situation, it's common to start looking for a new deal. The problem with this is when you constantly move from deal to deal it's hard to make wealth because you typically leave something behind each time you move. However, when you build on top of something else, you can generally go a lot further. If you truly know what's at your core, then your end goals will be aligned with who you are, and it will be less likely for you to drift into an ordeal. Throughout what follows, we'll build a framework so you can find what is at your core and keep your real deal, ideal. Finally, don't think it's too late to start; just start.

DEFINING YOUR END GOALS AND FINDING YOUR PURPOSE

The Cheshire Cat from *Alice in Wonderland* captures the idea of travelling without knowing your endpoint, when he says, "If you don't know where you are going, any road will get you there." One of the fundamental things to succeed in life is to know where you're going. The need to know where you are is equally necessary because, without your bearings, it's impossible to formulate a plan to arrive at your destination. Thus, the key is knowing both what you want and what you have. To help develop this path—navigating from where you are to where you need to go—a diagram has been included below.

How Power, Purpose, Passion and Principles Interact

Profession (Career) + Pursuit (Ministry) + Past-time (Lifestyle)

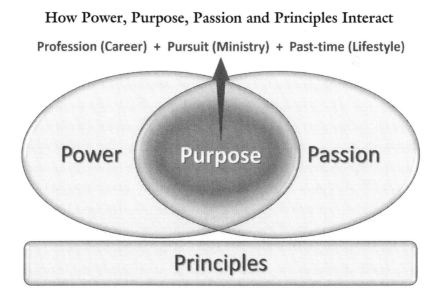

THE ROAD MAP TO YOUR PURPOSE: COMBINING POWER AND PASSION WITH PRINCIPLES

The above diagram acts as a concept map, where the different aspects of your life originate. These puzzle pieces of life generally fall into two essential circles, your Power and your Passion. Together they form the foundation of the diagram, with their intersection being its centre and most important part. This intersection is where your purpose is found. It represents all your end goals. Your actions and decisions in life should always guide you towards it, helping you find a path that allows you to flourish in life and be happy. But to understand it, we must now look at its components.

Power

The first section we'll consider is the circle in the diagram labelled "power." Power represents your strengths. Your strengths can fall into one of two different categories. The first category is your natural strengths, which are the talents and traits you're born with. The second category is your learned strengths, which are the skills you get from experience and education. This is where many people go wrong. They end up relying primarily on their learned strengths over their natural strengths. They get trapped doing what they've learned to be good at but do not necessarily enjoy or have been "wired" to be good at. They rely too much on past education—the courses they've been sent on and what their lives have led them to do—rather than what they were naturally born to do.

Those in this situation feel that they have invested too much time already and that they have too little time left to change focus to their natural strengths. They fear that if they attempt to change, they'll lose the time and work they've already invested. However, they fail to realize that by not adapting to encompass their natural strengths, they live life on a lower level and may never achieve the heights they could naturally attain. This is a painful lesson to look back on in your later years.

What's critical is to build on what you truly have, your natural strengths and learned strengths. It allows you to improve by maximizing the time you've invested already while laying the best foundation to optimize the future. When people align their work with their natural strengths, their work doesn't feel like such an ordeal; instead, it becomes something to look forward to each day because it's easy—it comes naturally. Aligning your work in such a way can be difficult without conscious thought, as these strengths are not always self-apparent. Often natural talents are things you probably don't even know you have, or don't know are special. They are things you may do without thinking and traits you might assume everybody has, but may actually be uncommon. Ask those closest to you, "What am I good at?" Ask yourself, "What do others ask me to do? What do they seek my advice on?" These often reveal your natural strengths, especially the ones you take for granted.

Passion

This moves us onto the second circle in the diagram, which is labelled "passion." Passion represents the things that you love doing. You spend at least eight hours a day at work, which is a third of your day, and over time this will add up to nearly a third of your life. You should be doing what you love at work because it represents such a large portion of your life. If you don't, you'll spend a significant amount of time doing something you dislike, and it will wear you down and drain your energy. Why, then, are so many people part of the "Thank God it's Friday" club? What will these people do at the end of the month? Will it be "Thank God the month is over? … the year is over? … my life is over?" Would it not be better to be part of the "Thank God it's Monday" club? It's possible to wake up in the morning and be excited—if you love what you're doing. Not only does working for something you're passionate about make you happier, but it also allows you to contribute more to your work. When you enjoy something, you can work at it longer and harder. It fuels you to stay the course through stressful and challenging times. You can get things done even when it doesn't seem possible because, despite the task being hard, you still enjoy what you're doing. This will lead you to get more done over time and, additionally, your enthusiasm will show in your work and make it of better quality. It now becomes easy to see how working in your passion can not only complement your power but also improve upon it.

Purpose

Where power and passion overlap, you find your purpose in life. When you can connect your power with your passion, you're performing at your peak potential. In other words, when you love doing something and you're good at it, it will come easy, and the results will be excellent. You'll get the feeling that time just flies and others will seek you out, be it at work or in your private life. The more you develop this, the better you'll become and the more you'll be paid! If you aren't regularly feeling this at work, you need to re-evaluate what you're doing. Even if you had enjoyed it at one point, this is a sign that your ideal may be becoming an ordeal. This sign alone doesn't mean the work you're doing is wrong for you or, by extension, that your ideal is misaligned. What it does mean is that something needs to change. Sometimes, it means you've slipped out of purpose and are focusing just on learned strength and money (the rat race). Sometimes you're still in your purpose, but you've forgotten why you're doing it and just need to reframe and find what made you passionate in the first place. Remember that life is simple: when you're strong at something and passionate about something, you're on purpose. It's important to realize that when you aren't on purpose, you won't enjoy life or what you're doing. You may enjoy it for a short while, but it won't last. Something will be missing.

Principles

Before unpacking more on purpose, you need to understand something critical: principles. You can't fully define your purpose without knowing your principles. Without principles, it's impossible to be successful. In the preceding diagram, your principles underlie the whole picture. Your principles are the core values that are important to you: your beliefs, your code of honour your priorities, etc. If your life and work aren't aligned with them, nothing else will matter. This is because when you break one of your core principles, you can't win. You'll self-sabotage before you can get anywhere. For example, if you (secretly) believe that it's wrong to make money or that rich people are bad, when a great business opportunity comes around that would make you a substantial profit, you'll subconsciously let the deal fall apart. You won't even know why it failed, but it will be your self-sabotage that stopped it from being successful. Going against your core values will only set you back, and even if you do manage some success, you won't be happy because the guilt of going against your principles will seep into your life. What's exciting, though, is once you understand your principles and get everything properly aligned, your life will explode through your purpose. When you understand your principles, you can use them to guide all your decisions—it makes life so simple and easy! Put these things together and life will really start to happen for you. Your principles and your purpose will always align, as both your power and passion are fundamentally entwined with your values. Once you have achieved this, your life and work are going to feel natural and everything will come together. Use your principles to navigate your passions and your power and decisions will become easy. You'll have a more fulfilling life and will find yourself living in your purpose.

UNDERSTANDING YOUR PURPOSE

Purpose has three aspects to it, which we will unpack in this next section. These are:

1. Your profession, which is everything to do with your job, career, investments; what you do to make money.

2. Your pursuit, which is everything to do with your significance in life, your ministry, charity, "give-back" and legacy; how you impact the world without making money from it.

3. Your pastime has everything to do with your lifestyle, hobbies, friends and fun; it's what you do that you enjoy but from which you don't make money.

These three aspects of purpose are more clearly revealed when we add a third circle (profit) to the first diagram, as shown below. It also explains how we get out of purpose, and the effects of that digression.

How Profit Influences your Purpose

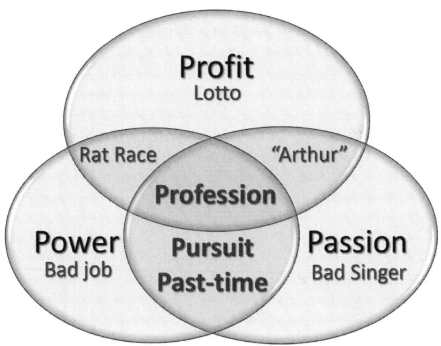

The profit circle sits much like power and passion, having its own space but also intersecting the other circles and making new quadrants. You can be in profit but not in power or passion. However, your goals and actions should always move you towards the centre of the diagram and into your purpose. Understanding the categories outside of your purpose will help you evaluate your situation and move you towards actually being in your purpose. Let's first look at these sections that are outside the central purpose section (represented by Career, Ministry and Lifestyle).

If you're only in your passion, you may enjoy something but aren't good at it, nor are you profiting. It's like being a bad karaoke singer—you love it, but no one else does! People tend only to do things in this section when they're trying out a new idea, hobby, instrument, etc. They usually aren't making money as they aren't good at it. So, it doesn't become a career and, typically, they don't stick it out as they aren't good at it.

You can also have money but no skills or passion. This is like being the lottery winner and is rare indeed! One must remember, though, a fool and his money are easily parted. So, this will also likely not last. If you're lucky enough to find yourself here, you better learn some money management fast!

Now, if you combine passion and profit without skill, you get the film character Arthur, the trust fund kid who loves his life but does nothing. This will also not last, as there's no meaning in that life. It's also a rare place on the diagram for someone to fall.

A more common area is when someone's good at something but not passionate about it, nor making money from it (or really poor money, perhaps). This is the bad job where you're working near minimum wage just to scrape by, even though you may be good at it. This is a fairly common quadrant, and there are millions of people around the world who live here as a means of survival. However, in most first world countries, people tend to move out of this quadrant as they realize it is a bad deal. They do so by moving to a new deal or by learning and improving their skills to get better at what they're doing and, thus, attract better payment.

When people find themselves in the quadrant of just profit and power but no (or little) passion, it's called the rat race, and this is where the vast majority of the population falls. This is the "Thank God it's Friday club" where people are working outside of their passion and are just chasing money. While people can earn a lot of money in the rat race, it's not a good place to be. These are the people who are always complaining or have midlife crises as their life is meaningless and miserable. They are the ones who go and buy a new car or boat to try and bring themselves happiness or meaning. Many people slip into the rat race without intending to. They start with something they love and are good at but end up chasing the money and building a career they don't enjoy but get well paid for. They become rich in money but poor in joy. Of course, this doesn't imply that all rich people are miserable. Not at all. The contented rich have excellent lives because they're working in their purpose.

THE THREE TYPES OF PURPOSE

When power, passion and profit combine, it creates the central quadrant known as career— or profession or prosperity—because it isn't just about the money, it's about excelling at what you love at work. Money is not the most important thing, but it's of considered importance with power and passion. It's a balance, which brings great joy and prosperity and makes the most significant impact in the world of work. Money is necessary because you can do a lot with it. You can use it to ensure security and stability for your family. You can also use it like great philanthropists, to do good in the world and improve other people's situations.

When you are working in your passion, on something you love, time flies at work. You also increase your abilities at a much faster rate. It's surprising how few people do this! Perhaps it's a throwback from school where students are told to work on their weaknesses so they can pass the exams. Life becomes a never-ending slog to improve what you're bad at doing. This doesn't work. You hate it, and you never get really good at it. If you work on your weaknesses (at work) the best you can become is mediocre. Companies and clients don't pay for mediocre. But if you work at what you love and what you're good at, you get better and better and become excellent. People pay a lot for excellence. Don't slip into the rat race; adjust your direction and get back into your purpose-focused profession. That's where you'll really earn, but you need to choose that direction. Your boss won't do it for you.

However, this still leaves us with one blank space in the diagram and the other sub-region of purpose. It's what happens when you link your power and passion but without profit (money). Some may ask if this is something to strive for. Is it also part of my purpose? Most definitely! The blank space I'm talking about is just as valuable as the profession section—it's just that most people don't consider it because it doesn't involve their "day job" and making money. It contains the following two sections.

Pursuit

Pursuit (or ministry) encompasses all the things you want to do in life (that are within your power and passion), and that you want to do to help other people. Think concepts like ministry, legacy, significance, and giving back. An excellent example of someone who lived their life in this section was Mother Theresa. She was good at what she did and she loved it. It was a life-work for her but it did not make her rich. Although this type of life is not for everyone, you must still have some things in your life that fall under pursuit. These can be all sorts of things, and they don't have to encompass all your time or be "world-changing." They can even be small, and seemingly insignificant. They just need to be what you can do to improve the world around you. It's what you do for others to return the good fortune you get from being in your purpose. This brings a tremendous amount of happiness and meaning to your life and makes a difference to those around you.

Pastime

The second section here is called pastime (lifestyle) and encompasses your life outside of money and significance. It includes things you love to do (and are good at) that make life worthwhile. Think of things like family and friends, hobbies, and lifestyle. For example, you could be a great parent or spouse, an excellent host and entertainer. You may have a hobby you love, like being good at gardening or painting and not make money from it. This is fine because of the enjoyment it brings you and those around you. And yes, these are part of your purpose too. Imagine thinking that being a great parent was not part of your purpose!

PERSONAL MISSION AND PERSONAL BRAND

Finally, your purpose will express itself in two ways: internally, it will be expressed as your personal mission and, externally, as your personal brand.

Your personal mission is what drives you and guides you through life and work. It will help you define the path you need to succeed. Your personal mission tells you what's important to you and will be formed out of your principles (your goals, priorities, beliefs and values). It will motivate you and will be the map to getting you where you need to be. For example, Oprah Winfrey is well known to all. Her personal mission has driven all she does. She is true to it and as a result she has grown a multi-billion-dollar business (brand). Her mission? "To be a teacher. And to be known for inspiring my students to be more than they thought they could be." She writes that, when she started, "I never imagined it would be on TV."

On the other hand, your personal brand will be how you manifest your purpose to those around you – how they see you. You will use this to communicate to others why you're doing what you are doing. It will also be how you use your purpose to sell yourself and the products or services you create. In turn, your personal brand will be essential to profiting from your purpose. Remember that this is what others see and they'll respond accordingly. Once again let's look at Oprah. Her outward brand is huge: TV personality, retail, advice etc. As one of the most recognized brands in the world, when she puts her name on something it transforms it into an overnight success. It's huge—but it wasn't always so. However, she stuck to her personal mission and created her own brand by being faithful to her way of living out her mission (challenging millions of viewers to live their best lives possible by understanding their own potential) even when others opposed her or said it wouldn't work. Sir Richard Branson has done the same.

Both are very important. Without your mission, it will be hard to get to where you need to be, and it will be easy to become misaligned with your passion and principles. Without your personal brand, it will be hard to be able to develop your power and, without that, it will be hard to make money or impact the world around you.

HOW DO YOU GET TO YOUR PURPOSE?

Now that you know where you need to be, you must now find how to get there. Andy Stanley said, "It is your direction not your intention that determines your destination." This is the principle of the path. Let's say you wanted to drive from New York to Miami. If your car is on the highway to San Francisco, it doesn't matter that you intend to go to Miami, you won't end up there. You're on the wrong path, going in the wrong direction, and it's your direction that will determine your destination, not your intention (what you want). Once you realize you're on the wrong road, it doesn't help to change your car, or to fill up with petrol or drive faster. None of these things change your direction. While these types of changes don't make sense in this example, many people still try similarly stupid sorts of changes in their life all the time. They try working harder or get a second job, but make no progress going towards where they want to go.

To get where you want to be, you first need clarity or to understand your intended destination. This is your purpose and your personal mission in each of the three different areas. Once you know where to go, the beautiful thing about direction is that you can change it in an instant. Furthermore, your ability to change direction means your past doesn't determine your future. Obviously the past does have an influence because it has brought you to where you are now. However, your past does not dictate or decide your future path. You really can choose where you want to be. You must, of course, realize that just because you change direction doesn't mean things will improve instantly—you won't just "arrive" at your intended destination. Just as if you had driven twenty hours towards San Francisco and then corrected your path to go to Miami, you'd still need to make up that time. But at least you're now headed towards Miami!

In changing your direction to your life purpose, you'll be on the right path, and one step closer to where you want to be every day. You're never too old to get where you want to be in life. Nothing will change if you keep moving in the same, wrong direction. The first step of getting anywhere is to decide not to stay where you are, then decide to change, then take action. If you make that decision now you can get almost anywhere in the next five years. That's infinitely better than a lifetime of regret and what-ifs.

MAKING IT HAPPEN

We all end up somewhere. Those who end up where they want to be do so on purpose. Everything worthwhile that exists begins with a purpose (personal mission) followed by a carefully crafted plan that is driven with massive action and the determination to succeed.

Many people don't understand their purpose, and that's where they fail because they don't get around to defining it. They have no clarity and live their life in doubt and confusion. Then there are people who understand their purpose, but it's just a daydream. They have no action plan or haven't decided to change direction and implement the plan. To make your purpose a reality takes not only a plan but also much work to execute. When implementing change, you'll always be challenged, and you'll need the determination to see it through and not quit along the way.

We must live our lives on purpose, as in the end, we only regret the things we did not do. A year from now, you'll wish you had started today. Don't put things off. Instead, say "I'm glad I did start today." In five years from now, do you want to be in the same place you are now? Or do you want to be at your intended destination? You can be. Start the change today, and live your life in your chosen future. Live on purpose!

To contact Tony Davis or find out more about how to live your life on purpose, email him at purpose@adavise.com